David Morris

The New City-States

Institute for Local Self-Reliance
Washington, D.C.

Portions of this material first appeared in *Resettling America*, Gary Coates (ed.), 1981, Brick House Publishing Co., Andover, Massachusetts.

Copyright © 1982 by The Institute for Local Self Reliance
2425 18th Street N.W., Washington, D.C. 20009 (202) 232-4108

All rights reserved. No part of this book may be reproduced in any form or by any electronic or mechanical means, including information storage and retrieval systems without permission in writing from the publisher.

Third Printing

Library of Congress Catalog Card Number: 82-82572

ISBN: 0-917582-49-7

Printed in the United States of America

CONTENTS

- 5 A New Way of Thinking
- 13 Energy, Integration and Recycling
- 16 Prevention Minimizes Treatment
- 19 Neighborhood Power
- 22 A Brief History of the City as State: Medieval Burgs
- 24 The City as Tenant: Nineteenth Century America
- 26 From the City Beautiful to the City as Entrepreneur
- 36 Development: The Cost of Growth
- 40 Global Corporations vs. the Municipal Government: The Rise of Economic Development Planning
- 51 The City as Nation: Inventorying the Resource Base
- 61 The City as Factory: Making It at Home
- 64 Localism and Globalism
- 70 References
- 72 Bibliography

A New Way of Thinking

> "Without power and independence, a town may contain good subjects, but it can contain no active citizens."
>
> Alexis de Tocqueville

The signs are there, harbingers of a new way of thinking. From the hills of Seattle to the arid flatlands of Davis, from the industrial city of Hartford to the university town of Madison, cities are beginning to redefine their role in our society. Long viewed as little more than real estate developers and social welfare dispensers, the municipal corporation is asserting the more important function of overall planning and development. Buffeted by natural resource crises beyond their control, cities are encouraging local sources of energy, food and raw materials. Burdened by deteriorating physical plants, cities are designing new, less expensive and more efficient life-support systems. Vulnerable to branch plant closings, cities are beginning to favor development that comes from within, that relies on hundreds of small businesses rather than one or two large factories.

The city is becoming an ecological nation. As such, the city maximizes the long term value of its finite piece of land by creating elegant, biologically-based systems. Local self-reliance is the goal. The term "local self-reliance" is defined in various ways by different disciplines. To the ecologist, local self-reliance means "closed loop systems" where the wastes of one process become the raw materials of another. To the economist, local self-reliance means capturing for the benefit of the local community the greatest amount of "value added" to the original raw material through processing and marketing. Local self-reliance, to biologist Russell Anderson is "a type of development which stimulates the ability to satisfy needs locally." It is "the capacity for self-sufficiency, but not self-sufficiency itself. Self-reliance represents a new balance, not a new absolute."

Consider the garbage we dispose of each day. Garbage is nothing more than mixed raw materials. The individual materials have a value. Once separated from the rest of the waste stream, the value of the material depends in large part on the degree to which it is processed into a useable final product. For example, a recycled aluminum can is worth about 17 cents a pound to community recycling centers (plus the indirect benefit of reducing garbage disposal costs). Compressing the cans into a smaller volume lowers the shipping cost to the central manufacturing plant, raising the value by 25 percent. Smelt the cans into ingots and the value rises again to more than 50 cents a pound. Convert the ingot into a consumer product like bicycle handlebars and the value of the aluminum doubles to more than a dollar a pound. The self-reliant city captures as much of this additional value as possible for the local economy.

"For business purposes the boundaries that separate one nation from another are no more real than the equator. They are merely convenient demarcations of ethnic, linguistic, and cultural entities . . . The world outside the home country is no longer viewed as [a] series of disconnected customers and prospects for its products, but as an extension of a single market."

President of the
IBM World Trade Corporation

The self-reliant city views itself as a nation. It analyzes the flow of capital within its borders and evaluates its "balance of payments." It recycles money much as it recycles goods. Every added cycle increases the community's wealth. Businesses are evaluated not only for the services or products they offer but for the way they affect the local economy. The results are often surprising. One McDonald's restaurant in a Washington, D.C., neighborhood was found to be exporting out of the area more than $500,000 of its $750,000 monthly gross revenues. Of the $35 million the 30,000 residents, businesses and local governments of Carbondale, Illinois and Northampton, Massachusetts, paid for fuels and electricity in 1980, more than 85 cents on the dollar left the economy immediately. As the mayor of Auburn, New York, remarked, "It matters little to us whether a dollar goes to Saudi Arabia or Texas. The effect on the local economy is the same. We are losing control over a substantial part of our own resources." "Stop the Leakages" has become a rallying cry for those demanding local self-reliance. Whether the leakages are raw materials dumped into landfills, or branch stores that take the majority of their earnings out of the community, or retired people who can't find places to offer their time and skills the result is the same—the loss of valuable resources.

This new way of thinking about cities defies traditional political classifications. It is ideologically neither right nor left. To John McKnight of Northwestern University, the liberal sees everyone as a potential client; the conservative sees everyone as a potential consumer. The liberal thinks people want services; the conservative believes we want commodities. Each agrees that the individual citizen is not the actor but the acted upon. Those encouraging local self-reliance have a different philosophy. The individual is seen as a producer of wealth and an active participant in the political process of resource management. Production rather than consumption is the explicit priority for self-reliant cities.

> "The conception of the city as a cooperative for the improvement and development of the capabilities and lives of its inhabitants is at odds with the doctrine of laissez faire and a national capitalism that has turned local citizens into consumers and so many free floating factors of production to be assembled and disassembled by the forces of the national market. The older conception of the walled city as a shared common enterprise has been weakened by the breaching of its walls and its transformation into an open economy."
>
> Norton E. Long, *The Unwalled City*

Self-reliant cities minimize government but not necessarily governance. The very terms "citizen" and "cities" connote political authority. Practically, as communities take an active role in promoting local self-reliance, the traditional distinction between public and private sectors begins to blur. A good example is Oceanside, a rapidly growing, conservative Republican city in southern California. Its citizens believe the community should take an active role in promoting the general welfare. The city has a significant number of retired people. With rising energy prices cutting into fixed incomes, the city council investigated the potential for using solar energy to lower hot water bills. Because traditional financial institutions wouldn't provide adequate financing for people to pursue this option, the city council unanimously approved a program that creates an alternative method of financing this income- and energy-saving technology. Homeowners lease solar hot water systems directly from private firms. The city helps to market the systems, guarantees them, collects lease payments and reduces red tape associated with permits, building code applications and the like. To participate in the program, the private firm must post performance bonds, agree to a consumer complaint process and charge less than a maximum monthly amount. Within 60 days of the commencement of the program, more than $15 million had been committed by private firms for investment in this city of 80,000 people. Thus, the city is not only capturing the value of an indigenous resource—the sun—but it is assuming an aggressive and innovative role.

Local self-reliance is an inward-looking process. But its dynamic may have a major effect on our national economy. By viewing themselves as nations, cities emphasize spatial considerations that undermine one of the principal tenets of our Constitution—the continental free-trade zone. The unencumbered mobility of goods, capital and people across state and city boundaries was for many of the founding fathers the chief purpose of the Constitution. By the late nineteenth century, the Supreme Court was striking down almost any local restriction on commerce as unconstitutional. Yet, a century later, localities are being given considerable authority to influence the ease with which we transport people, goods and capital across political jurisdictions. Cities have been granted the right to limit population growth, in effect limiting people's right to move. Cities enact returnable bottle bills, in effect prohibiting corporations from selling products in certain kinds of containers within the city's political jurisdiction. Cities require public employees to live within city limits. Cities favor local businesses over those outside the city.

The courts have been ambivalent about spatially oriented policies. Some municipal bottle bills have been overturned as unfair burdens on interstate commerce. Zoning ordinances that favor small businesses have been overturned as unfair discrimination to large firms. Growth limitation ordinances have in some cases been overturned when the courts concluded that the severity of the action had not been justified by the local conditions.

In an age of scarce resources the issue of spatial bias will not disappear. As we become more aware of resource flows, the justification of "place" as the basis for decision-making increases. For example, most states require municipal corporations to purchase products at the lowest possible price. Cities may not pay more for a product simply because it is produced locally. These laws were enacted to simplify contracting procedures and to reduce the possibility of corruption. But what happens when the advantages of local production become significant? Take the case of Carbondale, Illinois. It owns 110 vehicles. The city now imports 100 percent of its fuel. The vehicles could, at minimal expense, be converted to operate totally on alcohol. The alcohol could be produced locally from local waste products. Even if the price of the local alcohol were slightly higher than that of imported gasoline, the benefits to the local economy and, as a result, to the city through higher tax revenues would offset the price difference.

The new localism involves social as well as economic issues. To protect its citizens from possible runaway mutations, Cambridge, Massachusetts, imposed a six-month moratorium on research into recombinant DNA within its jurisdiction, affecting research at MIT and Harvard. The city of Morton Grove, Illinois, banned handguns. The momentum is growing as dozens of cities follow the lead of Detroit and restrict adult recreation activities to one small section of the community; New York City bans the transportation of nuclear waste across its boundaries; hundreds of cities vote in favor of a nuclear weapons freeze.

The new activism stems in part from a new generation, but mainly from a new context. In the 1970s, American cities had to deal with an unusually varied series of hard knocks. A prolonged coal strike forced many West Virginia, Pennsylvania and Ohio cities to deal with social tensions and even violence. Oil disruptions forced farm communities to seek alternative sources for diesel fuel, and New England and midwestern towns to develop programs to keep their elderly from freezing. The oil and coal developments in the western states spawned boom towns, sorely burdening the planning capabilities of localities. The collapse of the domestic automobile industry brought unemployment rates above 35 percent in some car-based cities. Floods, tornadoes, hazardous waste dumps, carcinogenic water supplies, the worst recession in 40 years, the harshest winter in modern times, are only some of the problems cities have had to deal with in recent years.

Another factor prompting a more entrepreneurial attitude on the part of cities is the increasing cost of maintaining municipal life-support systems. Simply stated, these systems were built for a different era. They are based on nineteenth-century technologies. The systems that provide us pure drinking water, safe and fast transportation, waste disposal, energy, heat and power have become prohibitively expensive. The subway system currently under construction in the Washington, D.C., area

Cities, by Population Size: 1960 to 1977

(Covers incorporated places of 10,000 population or more)

POPULATION SIZE	NUMBER OF CITIES			POPULATION (mil.)			PERCENT OF TOTAL		
	1960	1970	1977	1960	1970	1977	1960	1970	1977
Total	1,654	2,031	2,177	91.0	107.7	100.0	100.0	100.0	
1,000,000 or more ..	5	6	6	17.5	18.9	17.7	19.2	17.5	15.8
500,000-1,000,000 ...	16	20	17	11.1	13.1	11.2	12.2	12.2	10.0
250,000-500,000	30	31	33	10.8	10.7	11.5	11.8	9.9	10.3
100,000-250,000	79	99	104	11.4	14.1	16.1	12.5	13.1	14.4
50,000-100,000	180	234	249	12.5	16.3	17.4	13.7	15.0	15.6
25,000-50,000	366	474	536	12.7	16.4	18.6	14.0	15.2	16.6
10,000-25,000	978	1,167	1,232	15.1	18.2	19.3	16.5	16.9	17.3

Source: U.S. Bureau of the Census, *Census of Population: 1970*, vol. I, part A, and *Current Population Reports*, series P-25, Nos. 814-863.

America is a nation of cities, but not large cities. Less than ten percent of the total population lives in the handful of cities with more than one million people. More than thirty percent live in the eight hundred municipalities that are home to between 25,000 and 100,000 people.

will cost $2,500 for each man, woman and child in the metropolitan area. The five nuclear power plants owned by more than 40 municipalities in the state of Washington will cost more than $6,000 per household when, if ever, they are completed. A proposed tunnel under Chicago to reduce the backup of sewage into neighborhood basements will cost $1,000 for every resident.

Built a century ago, our industrial cities are wearing out. Two out of every five bridges are in need of major rehabilitation or replacement. According to *Business Week*, U.S. Steel Corporation is losing $1.2 million per year in employee time and wasted fuel rerouting its trucks around the decrepit Thompson Run Bridge in Duquesne, Pennsylvania. Street potholes have become a major financial drain on public as well as private pocketbooks. During the last seven years, more than 35,000 lawsuits were brought against New York City for damage related to street potholes and defective sidewalks. Some $161 million was paid out in compensation to plaintiffs, not including the costs of the city contesting the suits. A Chicago jury awarded one pothole victim more than a million dollars.

The problem promises to get worse. In New York City, streets which engineers say have about a 25-year life are being replaced at a 700-year rate. The replacement rate is 49 years in Cleveland, 50 years in Baltimore and 100 years in Oakland.

The 756 urban areas with populations over 50,000 will have to spend up to $100 billion over the next two decades just to maintain their water systems. Boston already loses more than 50 percent of its water through leaky pipes. Hundreds of homes in St. Paul find their basements flooded with raw sewage after a hard rain. Companies wanting to locate in certain parts of downtown Boston must bear the additional cost of a sewage holding tank to avoid overloading the system in peak hours.

Newer cities are not immune to these problems. Dallas must raise some $700 million for water and sewage treatment facilities over the next decade and more than $109 million to repair deteriorating streets. Booming Denver has begun informally delaying its repair and maintenance schedules.

All these factors combine to plague cities just as another combination of factors reduces their financial ability to respond. Congress has limited the ability of cities to issue tax-exempt bonds to finance certain types of development. Cities are borrowing money at such a rate that tax-exempt interest rates have risen almost even with taxable interest rates. Local and state tax revolts have limited property tax revenues, a major source of revenue to localities. At the same time, the "New Federalism" of the Republican administration has sharply reduced federal grants to localities. As proposed, federal expenditures for non-welfare programs will be cut by more than 50 percent by 1985 and welfare programs will be cut 25 percent. The cost is to effective local government. The National League of Cities found that half of all cities over 10,000 in population would have actual operating deficits by 1982. St. Paul, Minnesota, had to lay off 15 percent of its employees while Portland, Maine, laid off 20 percent between 1980 and 1982. Toledo, Ohio, has laid off 36 percent of its municipal work force in the last three years. No police have been hired in three years. No roads have been resurfaced in five. Garbage is collected every other week. The consumer protection program has been eliminated and the entire recreational system was shut down during the summer of 1981. "The parks were closed," says Mayor Doug Degood, "We didn't even cut the grass."

Even as the physical underpinnings of our cities deteriorate, the federal government is cutting public works money. This policy is particularly painful because the portion of federal aid for state and local public works had increased from 10 percent to 40 percent between 1957 and 1980. After having become accustomed (some would say addicted) to federal leadership, many cities are being asked to go cold turkey.

Yet, this reduced ability to raise local revenues is occurring as ever more responsibility is delegated to local governments. For example, the federal government eliminated direct financial assistance to low income families to allow them to install energy conservation measures in their homes and apartments. The federal government delegates that responsibility to the local community. No money accompanies the delegation of responsibility.

Federal aid reductions to individuals add to the burden on city budgets. One third of Newark, New Jersey's population receives some form of public assistance. "When the federal government cuts food stamp aid or changes the eligibility requirements for Aid to Families With Dependent Children some people drop out and look for local assistance," says Tom Banker, Newark's Assistant City Manager. "Our local welfare rolls have increased over the last six months. They had been dropping for three years."

In such an era, innovation and ingenuity are the best allies of cities committed to meeting the short- and long-term needs of their constituents. James Madison argued in favor of powerful small towns to encourage experimentation and diversity. If an innovation fails, the damage is minimal and all the other towns can learn from the failure. If an experiment is successful, the lessons of that success can be quickly learned by hundreds of communities.

The very number of America's cities virtually guarantees widespread experimentation. America is a nation of cities, but not large cities. Only eight percent of our population lives in seven cities of 1,000,000 or more. Thirty percent live in the 800 cities that have populations between 25,000 and 100,000. Shunned by the mass media that are headquartered in a handful of cities, these small- and medium-sized cities will be the laboratories of the '80s.

Energy, Integration and Recycling

The 2,000 percent increase in world crude oil prices between 1970 and 1980 adds to the burden of sore-pressed local economies. It also provides the motivation for a new conceptual model of the city. As gasoline, heating oil, natural gas and electricity prices soar, transportation becomes an important design consideration. The price of energy makes local self-reliance not only philosophically palatable but economically viable. Even as our school textbooks continue to extol the efficiencies of an integrated world economy, the rising cost of long distribution systems encourages us to think again. No longer is it economical to build a house with glue imported from one continent, wood from another, nails from another and fixtures from still another, to heat it with fuel that comes from still another part of the world, and to bring in water and electricity from several hundred miles away.

To illustrate the rising importance of distribution, today it costs twice as much to get food to our tables as it does to grow the food. Integration rather than separation will become the design criteria of the '80s. Rather than raise a tomato in California and eat it in Boston we will raise vegetables in Boston, in greenhouses warmed by waste heat from nearby factories or buildings. Small-scale steel mills (the industry calls them mini-mills, or even neighborhood mills) already compete with conventional mills 10 times their size because they use locally available scrap metal. After an exhaustive study to ascertain how it could save energy, Portland, Oregon, concluded that a five percent savings could be accomplished simply by reviving neighborhood grocery stores. Once again integrating business and residence we can avoid the need to require a resident who wants a pack of cigarettes, a loaf of bread or a gallon of milk to drive a two-ton automobile to a regional shopping center.

"The necessity of goods transport is a sign of failure."

Ernest Schumacher

Energy efficiency also encourages recycling. To make an aluminum can out of the original bauxite ore requires eight times the energy required to recycle an aluminum can. Similar savings come from recycling paper or other materials. In fact, the energy crisis may be considered a part of a larger materials crisis. Petroleum, natural gas and uranium are scarce, but so are many of our widely used construction and fabrication materials. As the shortages become more pronounced, the marketplace finds recycled materials more attractive.

A city of the size of San Francisco generates about 1,500 tons of solid waste per day. Broken down into component materials, San Francisco disposes of as much aluminum each year as is extracted from a medium-sized bauxite mine, as much copper as a small-sized copper mine and as much paper as is made from a good sized timber stand. The city itself is a mine. Its waste stream becomes the basis for new industries.

Manufacturing firms traditionally locate near their raw material supplies. Steel mills locate near iron ore deposits. Paper companies locate near forests. If our cities become mines for recycled material, we can expect industries to locate nearby. Since scrap remanufacturing plants are smaller and less polluting, they can be located in populated areas and serve smaller market areas. An aluminum plant using recycled metal requires ten percent of the capital as one using virgin bauxite. Steel mills using scrap can be built with less than ten percent the capital, and can operate economically at less than five percent the output of conventional mills. The same holds true for paper mills using scrap material.

Rising energy prices also encourage decentralized energy generation. In an age of political uncertainty, long distribution lines have made our communities vulnerable. Social upheaval in Iran brings gas lines to Toledo. Grand Forks, North Dakota, waits to see whether Canada will cut off its natural gas supply.

Cities have begun to react to this dependence by moving toward energy self-reliance. Oceanside and Davis, California, mandate solar hot water systems for new homes. Springfield, Vermont, expects to complete the construction of a hydroelectric facility that will allow it to export power to the same central utility from which it had been purchasing power for almost 30 years. Clayton, New Mexico, gets 15 percent of its electricity from a wind turbine and Burlington, Vermont, gets about the same amount from wood.

Integration again becomes the key design element. Fort Collins, Colorado uses the methane generated during the digestion of its sewage to fuel municipal vehicles and explores the potential for using the sludge as fertilizer for nearby cropland.

Cities whose bureaucracies have been fragmented now realize that there is a synergy to municipal development. When individual parts reinforce one another, the whole becomes greater than the sum of the parts. The city is an integral system. Its public works structures are part of its life-support system. The way it uses the land area, the kinds of economic activities it encourges, and the way it uses natural resources combine to foster the general health of the city. Municipal planning for self-reliance must take into account many factors previously considered outside the province of the municipal corporation.

This new understanding comes as we enter the electronic age. New analytical technologies and low-cost computers give communities a much better understanding of their environment. The new resource maps are dynamic. They track the movement of capital—money—across city borders. They analyze the composition of the solid waste stream, check the quality of the air, water and soil, estimate the costs of new development, identify where buildings are losing heat and evaluate the skill levels of the unemployed. The inward orientation of local self-reliance is complemented by the outward orientation of new communications systems. New technologies allow communities to horizontally communicate with others, to share information outside the mass media networks.

Thus, the global village becomes a complementary metaphor to the globe of villages. Cities become enmeshed in a global network of information while they use modern science to convert sunlight, plant matter and abundant locally available materials into useful products. Long-distance trade in materials declines, while trade in information, culture and knowledge rises. Electronic trade replaces molecular trade.

Prevention Minimizes Treatment

The new city-states must rebuild an infrastructure that is more compatible with resource limitations. Future city builders will have many fewer natural and financial resources to build the systems that deliver pure water, remove sewage and garbage, bring in fuels and electricity and allow for the transport of goods and people. Today's city designers must develop more elegant systems that are durable, yet flexible in the light of changing resources. As Ernest Schumacher once noted, the smart man solves problems, the genius avoids them!

One model of the future city might be Village Homes, a 70-acre, 200-unit development in Davis, California. The developer, Michael Corbett, stressed prevention. To reduce automobile traffic, each street ends in a cul-de-sac. The streets are narrow, half the conventional 45-foot width. Eight homes form a cluster. Homeowners are encouraged to fence their property facing the street, leaving the yards open to a narrow common strip between the two rows of lots.

A natural drainage system allows the soil to retain water after a storm and reduces the cost of sewers. Because the water does not drop below ground level, pumping stations are not required. Blocks in surface drainage systems merely raise the water level instead of stopping the flow. They are easily spotted and removed. "Each winter I get a pleasant feeling of warmth and righteousness around the Christmas season," Michael notes contentedly, "As storm drains back up and pumps fail in other parts of Davis, Village Homes is beautiful with its multitude of little streams and waterfalls."

Village Homes made believers out of private developers because its design saves money. Natural drainage systems save $800 per building site. Narrow streets reduce construction costs and open up more land for development. It was more difficult to convince city departments. The city engineer disapproved natural drainage systems. The fire department disapproved narrow streets. The police department disapproved cul-de-sacs. Over departmental objections, the city planning commission and city council approved the project, responding to pressures from a political constituency mobilized in large part by graduate students of ecology at the University of California. On a citywide scale, prevention can secure huge savings.

While Chicago attempts to attract billions of dollars in federal aid to build gigantic tunnels under the city to divert rainfall that clogs up sewer systems, a neighborhood-based organization proposes a simpler, prevention-based solution. The Center for Neighborhood Technology concludes that the central problem is that, as a result of paving over most of the urban land, almost all rainfall enters the sewer system at the same time. The solution is to slow down the raindrop before it aggregates. CNT recommends detaching rooftop drainpipes and putting splash blocks on the ground. It argues that delaying a raindrop is cheaper and easier than harnessing a flood.

The principle of prevention works as well in the energy sector. In 1977, the Seattle City Council voted to buy a ten percent share in two nuclear reactors to meet future electrical demand. A citizens' organization sued the city, claiming it had not looked at alternatives to new generating capacity. The city council agreed to re-examine its initial decision. A consultant was hired. Six months later, with the Seattle 1990 report before them, the city council reversed its vote and decided instead to aggressively encourage energy conservation. They found that saving a kilowatt was less than half as expensive as generating an additional kilowatt. Increasing efficiency prevents the need for expenditures for new capacity.

The dynamics of prevention are quite different from those of treatment systems. The more we prevent, the smaller the system, the less the capital expense, the greater the role for para-professionals, and the greater the citizen's involvement. Prevention systems, whether they be in health, criminal justice, or other social service areas, could preclude the kind of soaring costs seen in hospital treatment. Numerous studies have found that medical treatment does little to affect our overall state of health. Our life expectancy has lengthened as a result of improved diet and sanitary measures since the mid-nineteenth century. Since the advent of innoculation campaigns, modern medicine has done little to improve the general state of health. Studies demonstrate the inverse proportion between the amount of funding for control of diseases such as polio and measles and the incidence of these diseases. In 1952, there were 21,000 cases of polio, requiring the expenditure of hundreds of millions of dollars for medical care. In 1981, there were six cases of polio. The cost of immunization was less than $10 million.

Ninety percent of our doctor visits are for minor maladies which, although painful, will disappear in a few days no matter what the physician does. A growing proportion of people now visit emergency rooms of big city hospitals to get emotional support and reassurance. Yet, they pay for the hugely expensive diagnostic and treatment devices hospitals have acquired. Neighborhood-based educational programs, with community medical clinics, and laboratories, all staffed by para-professionals at relatively little capital expense, can deal with 95 percent of all our illnesses. In fact, hospitals may already be pricing themselves out of the medical marketplace. By mid-1982, more than five hundred Emergency Clinics had opened for business throughout the nation. No appointments are needed. These clinics have sufficient equipment to stabilize a critical illness so the patient can be taken to a regular hospital. They earn their bread and butter on minor ailments.

Indeed, neighborhood and family cohesion might dramatically reduce one of our growing problems—mental illness. Eric Fromm once expressed confidence that an investigation would uncover a direct correlation between the disappearance of the neighborhood bar and the rise of psychiatrists.

The criminal justice system also illustrates the validity of these principles. The concept of neighborhood team police has proven successful. The officers are assigned exclusively to a specific neighborhood in which they also may live. They patrol by foot and get to know the community and its residents. In Dayton, Ohio, the neighborhood itself has become the police force. Working with the regular police, they intervene in family quarrels and handle 80 percent of the complaints. Halfway houses have proven their worth compared to prisons. The cost of keeping one teenager in prison is now around $15,000 a year, and the incidence of recidivism, that is, the teenager returning to prison for another crime, is high. Halfway houses cost less than half as much, and the recidivism rate is much lower.

Neighborhood Power

The principles of prevention rather than treatment, and of integration rather than separation, lead to a third basic principle of self-reliance—subsidiarity. As Daniel Patrick Moynihan describes it, "Th(e) principle is that you should never assign to a large entity what can be done by a smaller one. What the family can do, the community shouldn't do. What the community can do, the states shouldn't do—and what the states can do, the federal government shouldn't do."

Many studies conclude that the home is the best place for medical care. Lower incidence of infant mortality occurs when midwives attend home deliveries rather than mothers depending on hospital operations. The cost, both in dollars and emotional energy, is far less if we pay the elderly to stay in the neighborhood than if we ship them away to nursing homes. Hospitals are now permitting the terminally ill to die at home, among loved ones. The process is not only a fraction of the cost of conventional hospital care, but pulls the family, and often the community, together.

Today, the financial crisis of cities has led them to contract out services to private companies. Some are using neighborhoods as contractors. Kansas City and Louisville are contracting with neighborhoods to care for vest pocket and neighborhood parks. "The cost of sending a full crew to a remote area of the city to spend 20 minutes clearing vacant lots has become prohibitive," declares Milton Kotler of the Center of Responsive Governance.

The principle of subsidiarity reinforces the principle of integration.

Both reduce the most costly characteristic of urban life, its tendency toward separation. Both emphasize a sense of place. Both tend to move us toward a city comprised of neighborhoods where people can fulfill most of their basic social and economic needs. By doing so, they lessen our dependence on travel, especially travel by automobile.

Leopold Kohr argues that the number of people who live in a city does not cause traffic or overpopulation problems so long as these people live in relatively self-contained communities. The descendants of the medieval city-states like Paris and Bologna and London live in such cities. As Paris grew it could easily have suffered the disease of urban sprawl that characterizes Los Angeles. It did not because "the city stayed neatly divided into a multitude of self-contained small cities—Montparnasse, Montmartre, the Latin Quarter, as a result of each having its own nuclear cluster of churches, schools, theatres, convivial centers and city halls of such attractiveness that few had a motive for jamming up the streets with unnecessary long-distance traffic searching for business or happiness in areas beyond their pedestrian radius."

We perhaps forget that many of our big city neighborhoods were at one time cities themselves. In fact, in the early nineteenth century in Massachusetts, new towns were created when the walking distance to the central town meeting hall became too great.

Neighborhood authority stems from pedestrian power. Its advantages to the city as a whole, when weighed against the automobile, are varied and significant. Currently at least one-third of the typical city's land area is devoted to the automobile. In Los Angeles more than half the city's entire surface is devoted to vehicles. That land area cannot be developed. It is often tax-exempt. The cost of building and maintaining roads has become a major part of local capital budgets. By paving over large sections of the city, rainfall quickly overloads sewage systems. Vehicle exhausts and rubber from tires represent some of traffic's residues. They pollute the air and run off the streets to complicate the processing of sewage.

Neighborhoods constitute a source of strength only if they are cohesive. Cohesion comes in part from stability. Some cities have used their political power to stabilize neighborhoods by protecting their citizens from the upheaval caused by absentee ownership of housing and real estate. Once again, a sense of place is given precedence over the mobility of capital. Since the majority of most city residents are tenants, this attitude leads the municipal corporation to protect the stability of neighborhoods by imposing restrictions on rent increases or evictions. In Madison, Wisconsin, landlords seeking to significantly raise rents must file a statement to describe the impact such an increase will have on tenants. Tenants in that city can be certified as collective bargaining agents by the city's Rental Accommodations Board. Davis, California, prohibits anyone from buying a single-family dwelling unless he or she is willing to live in it as their principal residence for at least a year. The District of Columbia imposes a graduated tax to penalize the speculator who buys and sells properties quickly.

> "We must return to a scale of government which is comprehensive to our citizens . . . To date, the centralization of government has destroyed community self-management and citizen participation. We must reverse this trend and develop our cities along the lines of neighborhood government and inter-neighborhood cooperation."
>
> Senator Mark Hatfield

When California's Proposition 13 property tax limitation was approved by voters in June, 1979, they expected a reduction in rents. When they found that rents actually increased that summer, despite the tax reductions, a wave of rent control ordinances were passed by cities. One of the most stringent is in Santa Monica. Eighty percent of Santa Monica's 80,000 residents are tenants. Its rent control mandate immediately rolled rents back to 1978 levels. The initiative established an independent board to set new housing rates—based on a formula that considers only the property's original cash investment, not its current or leveraged value. It permits increases reflecting hikes only in taxes, utilities and maintenance. Any tax savings or write-offs a landlord may claim are offset by proportionate rent discounts. All evictions must clear the rent board first. The panel is also empowered to prosecute owners should it find them delinquent in their duties.

The self-confidence and aggressiveness of the municipal corporation on behalf of its citizens is a relatively new phenomenon. Yet this development has deep historical roots. To discuss the future, it is often worthwhile to explore the past, going back several hundred years to the Middle Ages, when in the embers of the Roman Empire people gathered together behind walls to form towns and political communities.

A Brief History of the City as State: Medieval Burgs

"I love cities above all."

Michelangelo

It is ironic that contemporary cities should again become leaders in a movement to redefine the nature of modern economies. The revival of cities in the Middle Ages was part of the economic upheavals associated with the transition from feudalism to capitalism. The marketplace was both their foundation and their reason for being. In 1283 in Beauvais, the fine was five sous for assaulting a fellow citizen, but it increased to 60 sous if the citizen was in or on the way to the market. Cities fought with kings, bishops and the landed gentry to gain acceptance of the basic requirement of any commercial enterprise: the sanctity of the contract.

The proliferation of free cities, given the primitive nature of communications, was astonishing.

> With a unanimity which seems almost incomprehensible . . . the urban agglomerations, down to the smallest burgs, began to shake off the yoke of their worldly and clerical lords. The fortified village rose against the lord's castle, defied it first, attached it next, and finally destroyed it. The movement spread from spot to spot, involving every town on the surface of Europe, and in less than a hundred years free cities came into existence on the coast of the Mediterranean, the North Sea, the Baltic, the Atlantic Ocean, down to the fiords of Scandinavia, at the feet of the Appenines, the Alps, the Black Forest, and Grampians and the Carpathians; in the plains of Russia, Hungary, France and Spain.[1]

The struggle for autonomy was a long one. Cambrai, France, made its first revolution in 907, and three or four more before it finally obtained a charter in 1076. The charter was repealed twice, and twice won again. The total struggle for independence took 223 years.²

But there was a fraternity of liberation. Cities shared their newly found wisdom. Constitutional advances developed by one town would quickly be passed on to hundreds of others. The charter of Beaumont became the model for over 500 towns and cities in Belgium and France. Cities held labor conventions. They made alliances and trade agreements. Fernand Braudel describes the medieval city as "the classic type of the closed town, a self-sufficient unit, an exclusive Lilliputian native land. Crossing its ramparts was like crossing one of the still serious frontiers in the world today. You were free to thumb your nose at your neighbor from the other side of the barrier. He could not touch you. The peasant who uprooted himself from his land and arrived in the town was immediately another man. He was free . . ." In fact, a German saying from that time proclaimed, "The air of the city makes free."

The medieval city reached a level of prosperity not again achieved until the nineteenth century. Florence, a city of only 90,000 inhabitants, produced art, literature and technologies that are still prized today. The average worker in some medieval cities in the thirteenth century earned more than his counterpart in the late nineteenth century in Europe.

Development took place under the watchful eye of the municipal corporation. The town association controlled individual commercial conduct with a thoroughness unmatched in history. It protected the worker from competition and exploitation. It regulated labor conditions, wages, prices and apprenticeships, punished fraud and asserted the town's interests against neighboring competitors.

The city and the corporation were at first synonymous. Cities had economic might as well as political authority. They often bought in bulk for their inhabitants, and set prices and wages. As one writer comments, "The city was a positive instrument of the public welfare, for it could not only proscribe, but also promote."³

Although by the seventeenth century the free cities of Europe had fallen into ruin, torn by internal dissensions and external rebellions, some of the tradition of extended municipal authority carried over to the New World. The Albany, New York, charter of 1686 illustrates the wide range of accepted municipal powers. In addition to the usual public safety functions, it had a monopoly on trade with the Indian tribes. It owned all vacant land within its boundaries and the council alone had the power to allow an individual to practice a trade or craft.

The City as Tenant: Nineteenth Century America

After the revolution, American cities were subordinated to the states. To presidents like Thomas Jefferson, who viewed an agrarian society as the basis for social harmony, cities were a source of problems, not benefits. Thomas Jefferson once called cities "sores" on the body politic. Alexis de Tocqueville, although admiring the small New England town, worried about the impact that larger cities would have on our political system. He called for the creation of a national army to curb the potential instability of these cities. Ralph Waldo Emerson summed up the nineteenth century attitude toward cities, "Whenever I enter a city I lose faith." As long as there was little concentration of population, there was little interest in and little need for municipal authority. The 1840 census showed only twelve cities with 25,000 residents or more, and only three which contained populations greater than that of Florence in the fourteenth century (90,000), one of the great city-states of that period.[4]

But rapid urbanization lay just ahead.

> Between 1830 and 1840 railroad mileage increased from 28 to 2,818. The first telegraph message was sent in 1844. In 1852 Otis invented the passenger elevator and the first Bessemer converter was put into operation a year before the end of the Civil War. Centralized business services became possible in 1867 when the first practical typewriter was developed. The telephone was invented in 1876 . . . The 1880s were boom times in building, as skyscraper frame construction was introduced.[5]

By 1880 there were seventy-seven cities with populations greater than 25,000 and twenty cities over 100,000. Philosophically, institutionally and physically, the nation was largely unprepared for what Adna Weber termed "the most significant social phenomenon of the century—Urbanization."[6] Social reformers had one all-encompassing term for the problems of the cities of the 1890s: congestion. In New York's Tenth Ward (Lower East Side) the density reached 900 persons per acre, over 500,000 people per square mile, possibly the highest residential density achieved anywhere in the world in recent times (the current density of Manhattan is 120 people per acre). The rapid growth in population, and extensive immigration and internal migration, as well as rapid industrialization coupled with "the great and novel experiment of the day, namely, universal manhood suffrage" alarmed and threatened local elites.

Cities had no existing authority to deal with the social turmoil resulting from these rapid changes. State legislatures repeatedly intervened in local affairs. The Tennessee legislature withdrew the Memphis city charter in 1879. The Pennsylvania legislature authorized the governor to replace elected local officials with state appointees in 1901. New York, Maryland, Illinois, Michigan and Missouri abolished the local police departments of their largest cities and established state boards in their place. Legislatures created new city positions, ordered salary raises and mandated pension hikes; they passed bills relating to the smallest minutiae of city life, such as the naming of streets and closing alleys. Massachusetts enacted 400 special laws dealing solely with the city of Boston between 1885 and 1907. New York's legislature passed 390 acts for New York City between 1880 and 1890.

The courts upheld any and all intervention by the state. In the eyes of the courts, cities were "mere creatures of their state legislatures." In 1868 Judge John Foster Dillion, in a case involving the city of Clinton's challenge to a state statute granting the railroad the right to seize, without compensation, as much of the city's streets as the railroad deemed necessary, set down the legal doctrine of the time:

> Municipal corporations owe their origins to, and derive their rights wholly from the legislature. It breathes into them the breath of life, without which they cannot exist. As it creates, so it may destroy. If it may destroy, it may abridge and control... they are, so to phrase it, mere tenants at the will of the legislature.[7]

26   David Morris

In 1907 Supreme Court Justice William H. Moody agreed, "The power is in the State, and those who legislate for the State are alone responsible for any unjust or oppressive exercise of it."8

The distinction between the municipal corporation and the private corporation was illustrative of the different standards by which public and private sectors were evaluated. By the 1880s, the private corporation had been cloaked in the constitutional privileges of any person, unfettered, with few controls. One contemporary legal observer noted that the new-style corporate law judged that the only social relevance of corporate status was as a means of promoting business. The counterpart to this conclusion was that business activity regulation was not a proper function of corporate law. In other words, corporation law exists to help businessmen to act rather than to police their actions.

Yet, this same period gave birth to a strong movement for municipal autonomy. In 1875, the delegates to the Missouri Convention for the first time gave local governments the constitutional right to frame and adopt a charter with a governmental structure tailored to meet their own needs, and with at least some powers to act without specific legislative authorization. By 1925, fourteen states had home rule provisions either in statutes or the constitution. Cities were rarely given as much authority as they desired, but on the whole these constitutional changes gave somewhat more autonomy to local officials.

From the City Beautiful to the City as Entrepreneur

The internal problems of the cities were at least as much a barrier to local self-reliance as were outside interventions. There was very little data available on the city's housing stock and demographics. City accounting systems were disorganized, and it was the rare municipality that could compare its own performance to that of other cities because their recordkeeping and budgeting systems were usually incompatible. The first city planning commission was established in Hartford, Connecticut, in 1907. Massachusetts, in 1913, required all cities with populations over 10,000 to create official planning boards. By 1922, 185 cities had done so. New York City was the first to adopt a comprehensive zoning ordinance, which involved the city directly in land use planning. By 1926, when the U.S. Supreme Court upheld their constitutionality, there were 564 cities with such ordinances, and on the eve of the Depression there were 800.[9]

Yet, planning was not a full-time function. By 1926, only 46 cities had planning budgets greater than $5,000.[10] City planning was restricted to planning for aesthetics. To a society which saw little role for the public sector, comprehensive planning was viewed as an unwise intervention by government.

One English writer at the time aptly observed:

> In America it is the fear of restricting or injuring free and open competition that has made it so difficult for cities to exercise proper and efficient control over their development. The tendency therefore has been to promote those forms of civic improvement which can be carried out without interfering with vested interests. To impose severe sanitary restrictions, to limit the height and density of dwellings, or to prevent the destruction of amenities on privately owned land, may all help to reduce the profits of the speculator—hence, if he has any influence over the local governing bodies, he will secure that nothing but what is absolutely necessary and legal shall be done in these directions. But to purchase large public parks and to develop civic centers adds to the value of the privately owned land and buildings in the city . . . .[11]

The Depression effected a revolution both in the role that government played in our society and in the relationship of cities to the federal government. Harrassed by the twin problems of rising relief expenditures and growing tax delinquencies, urban leaders were exposed earlier than the nation's governors to the need for massive action to reverse the deflationary trend. City halls around the country became the targets of protests by armies of the unemployed. City officials initially turned to state capitals for assistance, but rural-dominated legislatures and budget-minded governors opposed loosening the purse strings to assist "profligate" cities. Rebuffed at the state level, municipal politicians turned to Washington for help. A new organization, the United States Conference of

Mayors, was established to lobby for federal aid to localities. In 1937 the Federal Housing Act made formal the new relationship between the federal government and the cities.

The influence of the New Deal went further than direct aid. The new philosophy of government as an active force in the economy encouraged city planners to redefine their own horizons. The Urbanism Committee, of Roosevelt's Natural Resource Committee concluded:

> In fact, the entire scope and conception of local urban planning needs broadening. While the influence of the physical environment upon the economic and social structure of the community is everywhere in evidence, planning agencies and planners have been slow to recognize or to give proper emphasis to the social and economic objective and aspects of planning and zoning. Studies of the economic base of the community, its soundness, deficiencies and its prospects, and the need for a selective program of industrial development have been almost wholly overlooked. The pressing problems of housing have not received the attention from planning agencies it deserves.[12]

In 1940, the first housing census took place, providing city planners with their first real data base. In 1954 the Housing Act provided funds through its Section 701 planning provision.

The capacity of local governments increased dramatically in the years between 1950 and 1975. In that period the federal budget expanded by 700 percent; state and local government budgets increased by 1,500 percent. Between 1950 and 1978 the federal civilian payroll rose by 33 percent; state and local payrolls tripled.

However, with expanded budgets came increased dependence on state and federal agencies. The difference in fiscal autonomy between pre-World War I and Vietnam War era cities can best be illustrated by the following statistics. In 1913 nearly 80 percent of combined state-local revenues came from local sources. By 1970, 80 percent came from state sources. In the period from 1920 to 1955 nearly three quarters of local revenue came from local sources, principally the property tax. By 1971-72, state transfers accounted for more than 30 percent of total local revenue, and direct federal aid brought the total close to 45 percent. In 1967, federal aid constituted 50 cents for every dollar that the big cities raised. In 1976 the nation's largest cities received more money from Washington than they did from their own state government.[13]

Until the 1960s, federal aid was primarily used to complement and expand local and state planning efforts. Since federal aid was part of a formal partnership, there were often matching requirements.

The riots of the early and mid-1960s, however, illuminated the impact of the migration of the white middle class populations, especially from the older Midwestern and Eastern cities. The federal government provided money, not as a complement to local planning efforts, but as a means to attain national social objectives, in many cases over the objections of local governments. Thus, funds were, for the first time, given directly to community organizations and to low income groups, thereby bypassing the city government. Civil rights, and later, environmental criteria, were imposed on localities desiring part of the federal largesse. In return for compliance, the federal government began to give 100 percent grants, with no matching requirement.

Categorical and project-related grant programs proliferated, developing a crazy quilt arrangement. By the early 1970s there were more than 400 grant programs. Each city competed for a piece of the pie. There could be little long-range planning because no city knew beforehand whether it would be awarded the contract, or if its grant would be renewed.

Under Richard Nixon, dozens of categorical grant programs were combined into block grants. The Comprehensive Employment and Training Act, the Community Development Block Grant program, and the General Revenue Sharing program were established. Block grants represented almost 50 percent of the total direct money from the federal government to the cities. There were few strings attached to these allocations. They were distributed on the basis of formula, so that cities knew beforehand the amount they would receive. Although these programs were renewed every five years, and their regulations were often radically changed, they did provide a more secure planning base for local governments.

But he who pays the piper calls the tune. Once the federal government viewed itself as a vehicle for imposing national policy, the level of administration of the program mattered little. School districts, regional bodies, special districts, small towns, local public authorities, nonprofit organizations, neighborhoods—all shared in the federal largesse. By the late 1970s, no sector of the economy was untouched by federal funds. Neal Peirce could note, with considerable justification, "Today, virtually no town, village, township, county or Indian tribe in America is without direct ties to Washington, D.C. And there is virtually no function of local government, from police to community arts promotion, for which there isn't a counterpart federal aid program."

Planning departments had become grant writing agencies. James Gleason, chief executive of Montgomery County, Maryland, summed up the frustration of the local official when he remarked in 1978, "The federal government has absorbed so much of the government jurisdiction that (it) has become the decider of all programs, and state and local officials have become implementers of those programs. It's not what you think is good for your community as an elected official. It's what they (the federal bureaucrats) think. It makes a mockery of the elected franchise."

Yet even as the criticisms of federal aid mounted, the era of rising federal largesse was ending. Grants to state and local governments peaked in fiscal year 1978 at 17.3 percent of the federal budget. Local aid drooped to 15.8 percent in 1980 and the Republican administration proposed to drop it another 50 percent by 1985. Cities began slashing their labor forces. Many began experimenting with contracting out services to private businesses in order to reduce the municipal payroll.

At the same time taxpayer revolts swept the nation. Proposition 13 in California and Proposition 2 1/2 in Massachusetts severely limited the ability of localities to impose property taxes. Since property taxes typically represent 40 percent of all local government revenue, such tax limitations forced cities to turn ever more to states and the federal government whose chief revenue source is the income tax.

Another reaction was setting in against the complexity of the planning process. Even as cities began to introduce master plans to guide future development in an integrated manner, neighborhood organizations and private developers joined forces to curb the municipal corporation's authority. Neighborhoods criticized the city government for abusing its authority in favor of outside private interests. The development industry worried about the explosion of permits necessary for construction. One sympathetic environmental attorney declared in 1976, "A project that required one permit a decade ago could easily require half a dozen or more today." Each permit he believed, "represents a response to serious public concern about a particular issue." But their "proliferation may indeed provide grounds for serious public concern. The processes of negotiating a disconnected jumble of procedures may have become so complex as to impede achievement of both the protective objectives of permitting programs and necessary planned growth. The current political reaction against 'big government' may be a demonstration of politicians' recognition of the impatience felt by a large proportion of the electorate with the complexities of government regulation."

The Republican administration proposed "enterprise zones" as its major urban development tool. Such zones would be exempt from almost all local regulation. They would be beyond the authority of the municipal corporation. Stuart M. Butler, the chief theorist behind this concept, advised fellow planners that the primary feature of such zones would be their unplanned nature. "We have tried several decades of bureaucratic planning," he said, "and that has not solved our inner city problem. Now we may get a chance to see what unplanning can do."

Ironically, in an era where the very word "government" has taken on the most unfavorable connotations, the trend toward more governance at the community level appears stronger than ever. A new form of neighborhood government is emerging. These new governments are sometimes called "associations or common-interest communities," that is, communities in which a person automatically becomes a member of an association by virtue of provisions set forth in a declaration recorded in land records. David Wolfe notes that "The nation's developers, planners and public officials little recognized the implications of the association movement they were starting in the 1960s. But experience is beginning to demonstrate something broader in meaning than first perceived. Specifically, the community association is coming more and more to resemble a new, more local form of government." Today's condominium or homeowner association not only maintains and lights streets, but owns and operates recreation facilities and conducts recreation programs, adult education classes and child care programs. Many provide trash collection and some conduct their own public safety programs, including fire and police protection. These associations make decisions about public space. They impose architectural controls. In some jurisdictions the association also operates sewer and water systems. Indeed, the mayor of Ann Arbor noted in 1980 that "the traditional local government is finding, for the first time, a major competitor in the delivery of public services."

In 1979 a Pennsylvania condominium, rather than hook up to a citywide sewer when it had already installed its own, seceded from the township to become its own town. Recently, a Florida appellate court referred to such associations as a "democratic subsociety in which the majority prevails if its will is reasonabie and its actions not arbitrary or capricious." The issue was the majority's approval, through referendum, of the board of directors' banning of alcoholic beverages in and around the clubhouse. The lower court's ruling tended to favor individual property rights. The appellate court's ruling favored the rights of a formalized group with a public nature.

Whatever one's political philosophy, the 1980s will prove an exciting period of experimentation. Already both political parties have asked for the convening of a national conference on federalism. A new relationship between levels of government is evolving. In addition, the issue of "development for whom" and the relationship between the public and private sectors are being examined. It is to those questions that we now turn our attention.

Systems of Cities: Arkansas

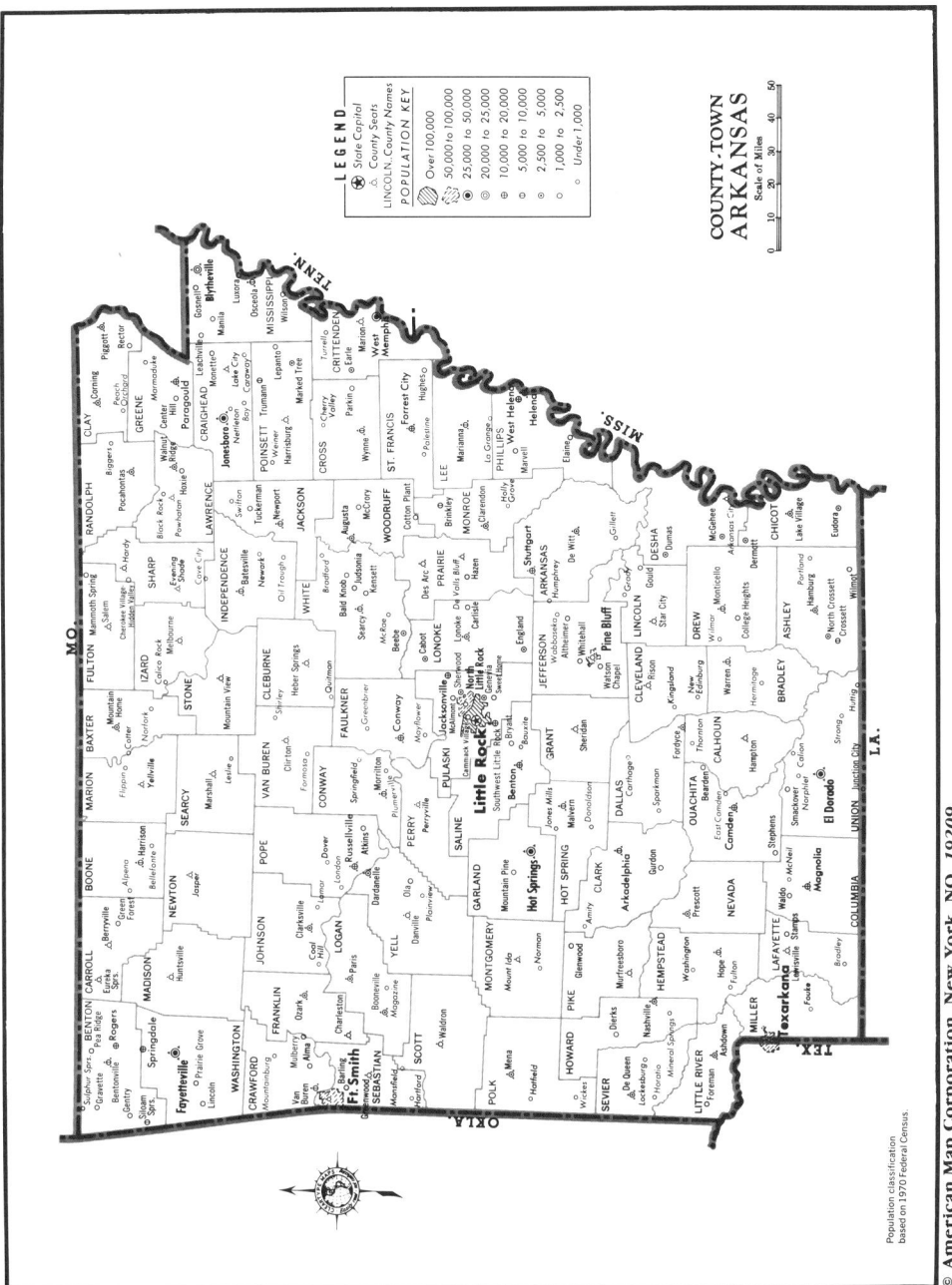

Arkansas' population resides mainly in small towns. Only 15 percent of the state lives in the one major metropolitan area surrounding Little Rock. And two-thirds of these live in Little Rock and North Little Rock. In the rest of the state only two cities have more than 50,000 people and only four others have populations greater than 25,000. The majority of the population inhabits hundreds of small towns, most of which have fewer than 5,000 residents.

Systems of Cities: Arizona

COUNTY·TOWN ARIZONA
Scale of Miles
0 20 40 60

LEGEND
★ State Capital   △ County Seats
GRAHAM. County Names

POPULATION KEY
- ▓ Over 100,000
- ◉ 50,000 to 100,000
- ● 25,000 to 50,000
- ● 20,000 to 25,000
- ● 10,000 to 20,000
- ● 5,000 to 10,000
- ● 2,500 to 5,000
- ○ 1,000 to 2,500
- ○ Under 1,000

Population classification based on 1970 Federal Census.

© American Map Corporation, New York, NO. 19209

Arizona's population clusters around one city—Phoenix. The metropolitan area contains half of the entire state's population. Because Phoenix retains its ability to annex outlying areas, more than seventy percent of the urban population lives in the central city. Phoenix and the other major population center, Tucson, were designed for the automobile and have some of the lowest population densities of any cities in the country. A chief characteristic of Arizona is its scale and the resulting distances between its network of small towns.

Systems of Cities: Illinois

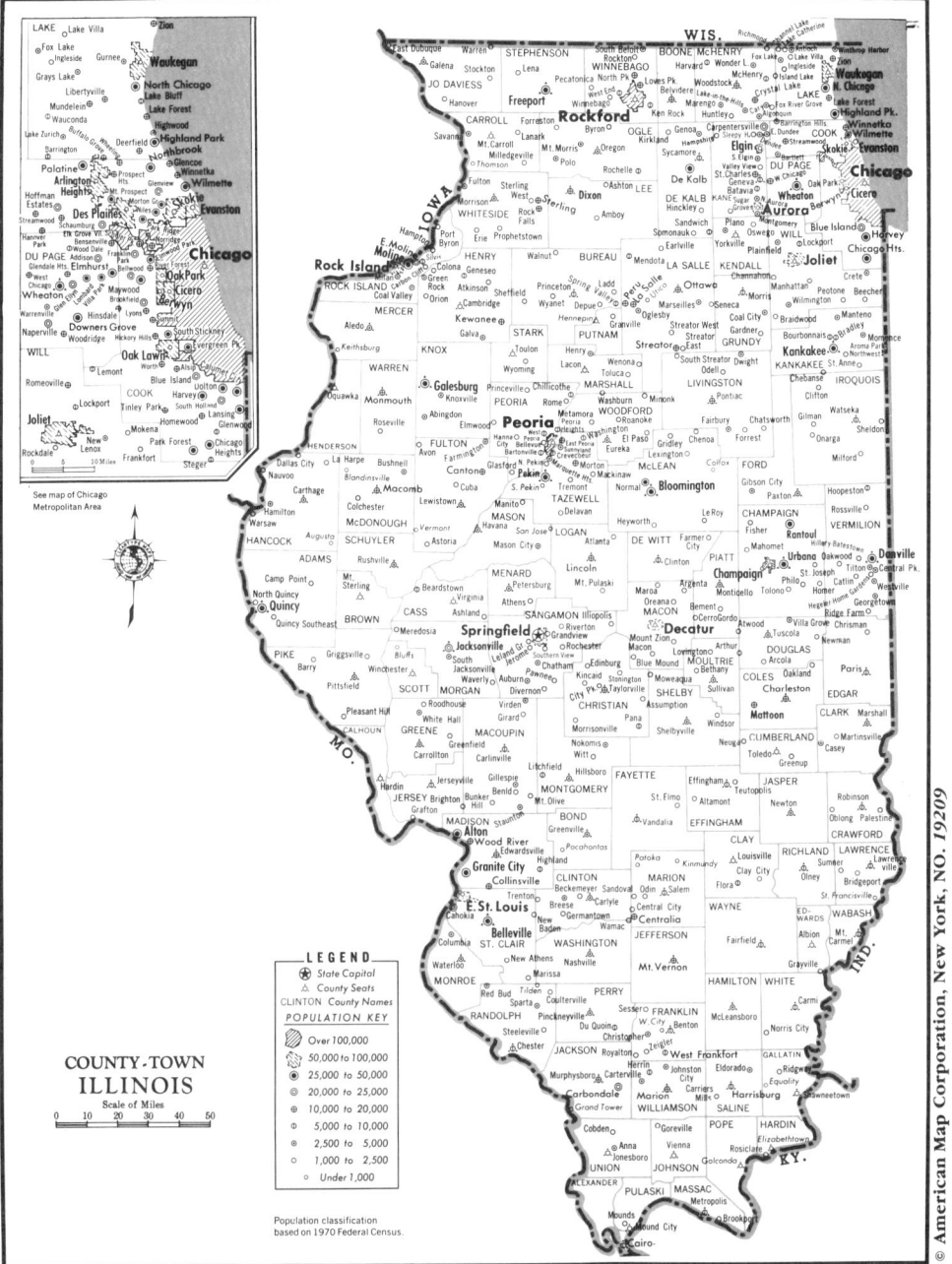

Illinois is dominated by the Chicago metropolitan area which contains more than 60 percent of the state's entire population. One of the nation's prime examples of a late nineteenth century industrial city, Chicago expanded by annexing outlying areas. Many of its neighborhoods were at one time independent cities. By the 1920s the extension of rail lines and the growing power of suburban municipalities curbed Chicago's annexationist tendencies. Today more than 20 mid-sized cities are located on the outskirts of Chicago, and only about one in every three people live in the central city. The rest of Illinois is dotted with a dozen widely separated mid-sized cities and hundreds of smaller towns.

Development: The Cost of Growth

> "The man who trades independence for security usually deserves to end up with neither."
>
> Benjamin Franklin

During the post World War II era cities were addicted to growth. Yet they found that growth brings costs as well as benefits. Environmental legislation forced cities to estimate the impact of growth. Increasingly sophisticated computer models permitted cities to monitor the flow of resources through their borders.

What they found was profoundly disquieting. One suburb of San Francisco, Fairfield, found to its surprise and dismay that total tax revenues from a proposed new subdivision would pay only half of the required new police services and nothing for other services. A 1974 study of Madison, Wisconsin, estimated the cost of a new acre of development was $16,500 for installing sanitary sewers, storm drainage, water mains, and local streets. The figure did not include the acre's pro-rated share of the cost of new schools, fire stations, arterial streets, wells, landfills, etc.[14]

When Proposition 13 reduced the property tax revenues for California's cities many began to add public development costs to the private developers' bill. Santa Monica had one builder include 100 units of low-income housing, a day-care center, a public park and incentives for the use of mass transit. Another developer was required to include a grocery store on the first floor of a new office tower to meet the needs of the elderly.

As cities gained sophistication in the planning process they began to reevaluate the favored practice of courting big corporations to locate branch plants in their community. As Neil Peirce noted, this type of development often had a negative impact.

When new industries are attracted from outside, they bring the well-advertised benefits of new jobs, orders for local suppliers, and a fresh infusion of money into a community. But there can be severe drawbacks. A firm with highly specialized labor requirements may bring its most highly paid workers with it. The jobs left for local residents may be few, menial or both. But local taxpayers will have to pay for new schools, roads, and other services for the newcomers. Capital investments to attract new firms have virtually bankrupted some communities—and even then they face the possibility that a big multinational firm may later decide there's even cheaper labor in Mexico or Taiwan and desert the area as rapidly as it came.[15]

The mating dance between cities and giant corporations had become too one-sided. One business magazine described the situation as a "rising spiral of government subsidies as companies play off city against city and state against state for the most advantageous terms."[16] Atlanta advertises its wares on Cleveland television programs and has opened an industry recruitment office in New York. In tiny Bossier City, Louisiana, the chamber of commerce encourages school children to write more than 900 letters to corporate executives telling them of the city's need for jobs, and its abundance of assets, such as clean air.[17]

When a city tries to negotiate with a giant corporation, it is a nerve-wracking experience, for it is a seller's market. The Detroit suburb of Trenton, population 24,000, gambled by refusing to give Chrysler Corporation the $36 million in tax breaks it had demanded in return for expanding its 4,400-employee engine plant. The City Council offered only $24 million because it felt the city needed the money for the school system. Edward M. Heffinger, mayor pro-tem of Trenton, nervously commented, "Our overriding concern was—what if we had guessed wrong here." Officials from Indiana, New York, and Ohio were waiting in the wings, wooing Chrysler. Finally, Governor Milliken of Michigan stepped into the fray, persuading the federal government to put up a long-term, low-interest loan. In this instance, as with most, the final resolution turned more on one's political contacts with the federal government, than with anything the local government could do.

Their self-promotional activities constituted the benign side of the competition between cities for corporate investment. Cities often used their right to seize land to put together a site large enough to lure a corporation and then, at its own expense, to install the physical infrastructure necessary to service the industry, and finally, borrow money, while writing off local taxes for 10 or 20 years as a further enticement. When the stakes were high, a growing number of local officials were willing to exercise the full authority of the municipal corporation to attract large plants, even at the cost of destroying existing communities. One of the best examples occurred when General Motors announced it would build plants in cities in Kansas, Oklahoma, and Michigan only if the local governments met its demands. Cities that failed to accommodate GM, the third largest private corporation in the world, were informed they would not be considered. Several cities, including Detroit, agreed to all conditions. According to GM, its plant there would generate six thousand jobs; in return, GM wanted the city to clear a 465-acre site. Unfortunately, the 465-acre site was home to many people—Poletown, as it was called, was predominantly Polish and had strong social cohesion. When 90 percent of the neighborhood owners refused to sell, Detroit used a recently enacted Michigan statute called the "quick take" law that allowed a city to condemn private property for public purposes and take title within 90 days, whether or not the value of the property for compensation purposes had been agreed on. In March 1981 the Michigan Supreme Court ruled in favor of the city and its Economic Development Corporation. The court ruled that the city was exercising its powers of eminent domain for a public purpose, the creation of "programs to alleviate and prevent conditions of unemployment." However, in this instance, in order to create a maximum of six thousands jobs the city of Detroit razed 1,300 homes, 16 churches, and 143 businesses, destroying an entire cohesive community.

Ironically, attracting outside investment may well increase economic instability. Absentee-owned businesses tend not to be good neighbors. They cut back employment during down cycles and recessions more than locally-based companies. They are less likely to purchase local services and products, such as legal assistance, financial consulting, capital borrowing and factor inputs.

The balance sheet of conglomerates is chillingly objective. Subsidiaries can be closed, not because they are losing money, but because they are not making enough. Said Joseph Danzansky, Chairman of Giant Foods, "But let's face it. Many stores are closed not because they operate at a loss, but because they are marginal and the capital can be more advantageously invested elsewhere." When Uniroyal closed its inner tube plant in Indianapolis, the *Wall Street Journal* noted, "Uniroyal could have kept the plant operating profitably if it wanted to, but under pressure from the securities markets, management decided to concentrate its energy on higher growth chemical lines... Many companies have grown too big to look at the small market." Peter J. Bearse, economist in New Jersey, adds, "We know in New Jersey that the average size of economic units in most lines of activity has been increasing steadily. We know that the largest firms' units are likely to move longer distances when relocating."

Cities are losing control over their capital as they lose control over their jobs and factories. In the late 1970s an older ethnic neighborhood in Chicago discovered that its residents had deposited $33 million in a local savings and loan association but had received back only $120,000 in loans. That discovery, made only after exhaustive and difficult research, led to the enactment of a federal law requiring financial institutions to invest a significant amount of their locally generated deposits in a local area. But no legislation could stop the hemorrhage of capital that accompanies the advent of electronic banking and money market funds. Not only neighborhoods within larger cities, but entire small- and medium-sized cities are now witnessing the largest outflow of local dollars in history.

> "Indeed, the concept of the local bank really makes no sense when once isolated cities are linked together by population corridors and when banking technology permits instantaneous transfer of money from city to city and around the world."
>
> Paul Nevels, Assistant Vice President, Texas Commerce Bank, Dallas

With the advent of electronic banking and money market funds, the problem of capital outflow hit every small city in the country. Money market funds, centered in the nation's major cities, withdrew money from small communities and reinvested it in national corporations or federal securities. Money market funds grew from $11 billion in late 1978 to almost $800 billion in mid-1982. The American Bankers Association estimated that 50 to 70 percent of this growth was at the expense of financial institutions—and many in small towns. Many small city banks and savings and loan associations, to preserve their own profitability and liquidity, invested their own deposits in money market instruments rather than in their own communities. Elmor Romines, President of Progressive Federal of Houston, Missouri, says, "It's like a pipeline with a valve in every daggum community in this country." To individual residents and local financial institutions, the money market fund was an attractive investment. Each received security and a higher interest rate. But the price was a lack of funds lendable to local residents and businesses. The *Wall Street Journal*, commenting on the trend in mid-1982 concluded, "If the drain continues, less affluent, slower-growing areas of the country will have a tough time financing their local communities."

Global Corporations vs. the Municipal Government: The Rise of Economic Development Planning

Caught in a vicious cycle, cities end up competing for fewer and fewer companies. In 1971, there were 12.4 million business enterprises of all sizes and kinds in America, including 3.3 million farms. Of that 12.4 million, over half (6.4 million) had gross sales of less than $10,000. Another 3.4 million failed to reach $50,000 in sales, and still another one million had $100,000 in yearly sales. Thus, nearly 11 million of the nation's 12.4 million firms, or 87.2 percent, had sales of less than $100,000 in that year.[18]

On the other hand, less than one percent of the service firms had multistore operations. Of the 275,000 manufacturing companies in the United States about 10 percent had more than 99 employees.[19] Three companies sold 80 percent of the cold breakfast cereal in 1975. Three companies sold 80 percent of the home insulation in that year. Four sold 70 percent of the dairy products. One sold 90 percent of the canned soups.[20] Fewer than 30 giants owned over 20 percent of the cropland. Eight oil companies controlled 64 percent of proven oil reserves, 44 percent of uranium reserves, 40 percent of coal under private lease, and 40 percent of copper deposits.[21]

Yet it turns out that small businesses, not the giant corporations, are the backbone of local economies. A massive study of 5.6 million firms (representing 82 percent of the nation's private jobs) was conducted by David Birch. He tracked these firms over a seven-year period, from 1971 to 1978, and concluded that the country's biggest job producer was small firms. Two-thirds of all new jobs were created in companies employing fewer than 20 people. The top 1,000 firms on the *Fortune* list generated only 75,000 jobs, or just a little more than 1 percent of all new jobs created between 1970 and 1976.[22] Birch found that most jobs came from the start-up of new firms, and the expansion of existing small businesses, destroying the myth that economic development is created by plant relocations and expansion by big corporations.

These figures gave an ironic twist to the frenzied competition among cities for giant plant locations. Cities, built on a foundation of thousands of small businesses, often found themselves in the position of forcing out small firms in order to make room for a branch of a larger corporation.

By the end of the 1970s, cities were beginning to understand the nature of their dilemma. They began to directly involve themselves in economic developments. In 1974 the Housing and Community Development Act provided Community Development Block Grants (CDBG), lump sum payments to cities which enabled them to coordinate community development and economic development planning. The 1977 amendments to this act expanded the economic development activities permitted under the CDBG program.

Increased funds and authority gave rise to dozens of local economic development corporations, with the power to acquire land, lease land, construct buildings and provide short and long term financing to businesses.

Cities directly control vast human, physical and financial resources. There are at least seven counties or cities in California that have over $100 million in public pension funds. The city of Washington, D.C., owns over 4,000 buildings and hundreds of acres of land.

Cities have an important lever in encouraging local small business development: government purchasing. The dollar volume of state and local government purchasing has grown dramatically in the past decade, and it now exceeds that of the federal government. In 1963, the federal government spent approximately two-thirds of all money spent by all levels of government for goods and services. In 1973, state and local governments spent $75.7 billion on purchases of goods and services, some 50 percent more than the federal government.

Selected Municipal Pension Funds — 1978
(All figures are in Millions $, at market value.)

Name of Fund	Total Assets	Common Stock	Preferred Stock	U.S. Government Securities	Corporate Bonds	Mortgages	Cash & Short Term Investments	Other
City of Albany Pension Trust	$9.1	$2.5	$.05	$—	$3.49	$1.15	$1.9	$—
Amarillo Board of Firemen Relief and Retirement Fund	$4.4	$1.2	$.05	$.67	$2.21	$—	$.2	$.10
Fire and Police Employees Retirement System of Baltimore	$216.3	$43.5	$1.9	$26.38	$9.13	$8.77	$37.1	$11.13
Baltimore City	$215.2	$30.4	$1.96	$26.37	$96.13	$8.77	$37.0	$9.00
City of Birmingham Retirement and Relief System	$79.9	$11.5	$.62	$27.56	$12.84	$5.80	$18.1	$3.46
Dallas Police, Fire & Fire Alarm Operators Pension Fund	$70.6	$33.2	$.59	5.04	$16.03	$—	$15.7	$—
Denver Public School Employees' Pension & Benefit Association	$212.9	$3.8	$—	$26.02	$110.56	$70.47	$2.1	$—

City of Detroit-Policemen & Firemen Retirement System	$48.0	$90.9	$—	$22.41	$142.21	$22.51	$73.4	$132.48
Employees' Retirement System, City of Norfolk, Virginia	$62.4	$19.2	$.49	$13.60	$24.40	$.33	$4.43	$—
Oakland Municipal Employees' Retirement System	$36.8	$9.5	$1.08	$3.39	$7.54	$.70	$.80	$13.77
Oakland Police & Fire Retirement Systems	$60.8	$10.2	$.24	$12.92	$27.19	$—	$6.65	$3.57
City Employees Consolidated Pension Fund, Ocala, Florida	$4.5	$1.4	$.06	$—	$2.57	$—	$.65	$—
Employees Retirement System of Oklahoma City	$11.7	$2.4	$.04	$2.93	$6.18	$—	$—	$—

Pension funds are particularly well-suited as a source of capital for long-term investments. Most cities do not directly control their public employees' retirement funds. In most states local pension funds are linked directly into state pension funds and controlled at the state level. Strict regulations control the types of investments public pension funds can make. Several cities, including Philadelphia and San Jose, have used local pension funds to assist local residents in buying homes.

Selected Municipal Pension Funds — 1978
(All figures are in Millions $, at market value.)

Name of Fund	Total Assets	Common Stock	Preferred Stock	U.S. Government Securities	Corporate Bonds	Mortgages	Cash & Short Term Investments	Other
City of Providence Employees' Retirement System	$56.7	$28.6	$.50	$2.90	$19.53	$2.66	$—	$2.55
City of Saginaw Policemen and Firement Retirement System	$15.2	$3.4	$—	$.89	$11.72	$—	$.27	$—
Policemens' Pension Fund of the City of St. Petersburg	$9.0	$.9	$—	$1.66	$1.03	$—	$5.35	$—
Firemen's Pension Fund of the City of St. Petersburg	$5.8	$.6	$—	$1.22	$.53	$—	$3.39	$—
City of San Antonio Fire and Police Pension Fund	$37.8	$17.0	$9.24 (bk)	$.06	$3.71	$6.93	$.85	$—

Duluth Teachers' Retirement Fund Association	$27.5	$8.6	$—	$2.86	$5.63	$1.84	$.84	$—
Firefighters' Pension System of Kansas City, MO	$27.8	$10.9	$—	$1.78	$13.69	$—	$1.19	$.18
The Employees' Retirement System of Kansas City, MO	$39.4	$15.2	$.009	$4.67	$17.89	$—	$1.40	$.18
Los Angeles Fire & Police Pension System	$565.4	$114.8	$—	$79.07	$265.70	$—	$76.25	$29.56
Newport News Employees' Retirement Fund	$32.9	$11.9	$.25	$5.34	$8.31	$.29	$6.82	$—

Source: Pension World, Vol. 14, No. 4, April 1978, Atlanta, Ga.

This abundance of resources is now combined with expanded municipal authority. The judicial system has accepted the right of cities to favor local commerce. Several local governments favor local suppliers. Detroit and Livermore, California, have purchasing provisions awarding contracts to local suppliers even if they bid up to 5 percent higher. The state legislature in Maine mandates that state institutions such as penal institutions, vocational and technical schools and state hospitals purchase food produced locally, even if it is 5 percent higher in price. In Washington, D.C., the city government is required to purchase 25 percent of all its goods and services from local, minority-owned firms.

Cities are also wanting to leverage their own government bank accounts to benefit the local economy. Until the 1970s, even large cities that deposited hundreds of millions of dollars in local banks imposed no conditions on these deposits. In many cases, the cities earned little interest and the vast majority of the money was loaned outside of the community. By 1982, a number of cities, like the District of Columbia and Santa Monica, required financial institutions in which they deposited their money to re-invest this money in local mortgages or consumer loans. These cities still received the same return on their deposits as they would in any bank, but were able to channel the capital into projects that benefit the local economy.

The municipal budget is only a small part of the powers the municipal corporation can exercise on behalf of its citizens. The bonding capacity of cities is often much larger than their budgets, giving them the ability to develop long-term construction projects and provide low-interest loans for economic development purposes. In fact, between 1970 and 1978 the dollar volume of new debt for municipalities was about double the total issuance of all corporate debt.

Sometimes the city itself operates a business. Cities since the turn of the century have owned and operated energy, water, sewage and transportation utilities. Cities have been involved in other business enterprises, but the courts have not always upheld the city's determination of what constituted a "public purpose." The Arizona and Oklahoma constitutions specifically grant municipal corporations the right to engage in business. Relatively new undertakings such as low-rent housing, airports, off-street parking facilities, have gained acceptance as public purposes by the courts. Less often, approval has been given to such commercial undertakings as hotels, restaurants, and liquor stores. Cities in Ohio have been permitted to own a railroad that operates outside municipal limits. Thirty cities own their own cable television systems.

However, the new generation of city leaders tends to believe less in direct municipal ownership than they do in the city as an overall economic planner, the mechanism that establishes the rules for private investment and channels resources into those areas of the local economy that would most effectively benefit large segments of the local population. Thus, the economic development authority of Dayton provides funds to cooperatives. In Eugene, the city uses money to establish a neighborhood-owned, community land trust and the city council in Madison puts up $50,000 to attract conventions to local hotels. There, the local Chamber of Commerce matched one dollar for every two put up by the city.

The municipal corporation has radically changed its functions from the days when the "city beautiful" was its primary concern. Economists discuss "foreign" and "domestic" policy in relation to central city areas. The state of the art of urban economic development has moved from simple business promotion to targeted intervention in the local economy based on economic research and planning. It then moved to more entrepreneurial investments and business development and financial leveraging. Formerly little more than a handmaiden to private real estate developers, the municipal corporation began to exercise its authority to encourage the best social use of its land, not only the use that would generate the greatest private profit. James Rouse, one of the nation's largest real estate developers commented, "It's very clear that we are in the midst of probably the most radical change in our concept of private property that we have ever seen in this country. The notion that a developer has a right to develop because he owns a piece of land and the public must let him is rapidly changing."

The new entry of cities into economic development ventures increasingly has led to joint ventures with private firms. Ralph Guthrie, President of the Council for Urban Economic Development, an organization which doubled its membership between 1978 and 1980, remarked, "economic development planning is the way of the future for city planning. We have no choice. With federal funds drying up our partnership with the private sector is the way we must go." Baltimore Mayor Donald Schaefer argued, "decentralization and development at the local level are becoming increasingly important. These new public-private partnerships mean a new type of deal making and risk taking."

The boundary line between public and private is a fuzzy one, and evolves as the society changes. One Minnesota high court noted, "the need for local power grows with the complexity of modern life and the population."[23] A court of appeals wrote, "As a commonwealth develops politically, economically, and socially, the police power likewise develops within reason to meet the changed and changing conditions."[24] Still another judge noted, "economic and industrial conditions are not stable. Times change. Many municipal activities, the propriety of which are not now questioned, were at one time thought, and rightly enough so, of a private character."[25]

The interplay of the private and public sector is nowhere more evident than in the land use restrictions which state and local governments have imposed on private development. A most revealing set of restrictions is the Vermont Land Use and Development Law enacted in 1970. Nine district environmental councils oversee a population about that of a small-sized city. The Chittenden Environmental Council denied a permit to a regional shopping mall containing 80 stores and 440,000 square feet of commercial space, in the town of Williston. The reason was that the store would reduce tax revenues of the city of Burlington, causing the state to compensate it for some of the lost tax revenues which would have supported the educational system. This development was denied because it would draw away commerce from neighboring towns, reducing the tax base for the local government.

In short, the municipal corporation is an evolving creature. Once viewed as nothing more than a "mere tenant," cities now possess immense economic and political authority. They are still subordinate to the state legislatures. But in an increasing number of states, the burden of proof that they can exercise power is no longer on the cities, but on the states to prove they can't. Forty-one states had home rule provisions by 1975, either as part of their constitutions, or by statute. Some, such as Maryland, Alaska, and New York, used language such as is in the Tenth Amendment to the U.S. Constitution. Before home rule, cities could exercise no powers that were not explicitly given them by the state legislatures. Under many home rule provisions, cities can exercise any powers which are not explicitly denied them.

Because of complex legal rulings, municipal authority has not been expanding linearly. Recent judicial decisions indicate a reluctance to give the municipal corporation unlimited powers. In January 1982 the United

States Supreme Court overruled a lower court, deciding that the city of Boulder, Colorado, had violated anti-trust statutes in a case involving a privately owned cable T.V. company. The case was important because in 1943 the Supreme Court had said states were generally to be considered exempt from federal anti-trust laws under the theory that they have special regulatory powers protected in the Constitution under the concept of federalism. Boulder argued that cities with home-rule governments sanctioned by state legislatures automatically shared that immunity. The Supreme Court said no. Justice Brennan, writing the 5-3 majority opinion, said that the state anti-trust exemption embodies "the federalism principle that the states possess a significant measure of sovereignty under our Constitution. But this principle contains its own limitation. Ours is a 'dual system of government' which has no place for sovereign cities..." A state could delegate its anti-trust exemption to localities but it could not be assumed through a generalized grant of home-rule authority.

The thrust of the New Federalism as conceived by the Republican administration will still further complicate the issue of local authority. Conservatives appear ambivalent as to whether they prefer to delegate authority to lower levels of government or wield the federal authority to curb the exercise of power at any level. The Department of Transportation attempted to preempt the authority of New York City to regulate the transport of radioactive waste through its jurisdiction. The courts ruled in favor of New York. The White House Commission on Housing proposed federal regulations cutting off federal housing assistance to cities that institute rent controls. The Senate almost enacted a law prohibiting cities from regulating cable television systems. At the last moment, the law was sent back to committee for further deliberations. Where the new administration genuinely wants to delegate authority, the power is to be given to the states, not the cities. That attitude is consistent with the Constitution which doesn't mention cities at all. But it is inconsistent with current demographic realities. The Administration argues, and the governors agree, that state governments in the last 20 years have become modern and sophisticated. No longer the rotten bourough of the American political system, they now have the capability to meet the needs of the time. Moreover, the one-man one-vote judicial decision of the 1960s eliminated the lopsided, rural state legislative majorities in urbanized states.

Still, urban dwellers are worried that such a transfer of power back to the states would be harmful to their interests. The fear is especially strong in smaller cities. These have never had the political clout or lobbying strength of the larger municipalities. Rather than receiving direct federal aid, as has been the case since the mid-1970s, under the New Federalism, these cities would compete with one another and with more rural communities for aid from state governments.

Overlapping the issue of the prerogatives of each level of government is the issue of the relationship between the private corporation and the public corporation.

In ancient Greece a citizen was considered a shareholder rather than a taxpayer. At the beginnings of this nation no distinction at all was made between a business and a city. By the end of the nineteenth century the pendulum had swung to the other extreme. Cities had almost no right to regulate or operate private businesses. Today the courts and the country are trying to find a reasonable path between these two poles.

This philosophical issue becomes all the more difficult to resolve because since World War II another form of corporation—the public authority—has grown to prominence. Begun by Franklin Roosevelt as a principal tool for implementing his massive public works programs, by 1958 the Federal Reserve Bank of Philadelphia aptly described "Pennsylvania's Billion Dollar Babies" as "not quite governments and not private businesses. Paradoxically, they are born of government, yet not directly controlled by the electorate. Nourished by business methods, they are nonprofit, have no stockholders, and are immune from anti-trust laws. They build public projects using private money. They operate public utilities yet they are not regulated by Public Utilities Commissions." They are, in the words of one urban analyst, "corporations without stockholders, political jurisdictions without voters or taxpayers."

Public authorities are not tiny parts of the political system. They are central to it. They are the largest category of borrowers in the tax exempt bond market, raising more money for capital investment than all state or municipal governments. Ann Marie Haucks Walsh, an expert on these unelected governments, expresses the fear that they wield "a massive influence on the patterns of development in the nation," an influence "that is largely insulated from public debate."

Thus, the power of the municipal corporation is not absolute. But the analytical tools and technologies at its disposal are greater than ever before in history. Armed with the knowledge that small business is the catalytic force in the local economy, understanding their resource flows better than at any other time in history, imbued with the determination of a generation matured during difficult social times, our municipal corporations are now beginning to tackle their problems with increasing initiative and innovation. The energy crisis, which has confronted cities with the possibility of rationing, shortages, serious economic dislocation, and reduced budgets, reinforces the need to operate more efficiently and productively. As we enter the 1980s, one central issue remains. How far can our cities go toward achieving self-reliance? Can we realistically conceive of the city as a nation, producing a significant amount of its goods and services?

The City as Nation: Inventorying the Resource Base

"At the end of the last century and early in this, the South Bronx was a garden community centered on the new, fortress-like building of the American Bank Note Company whose employees cultivated their own gardens on company land. The Bank Note Company is still there, its fortress aspect more grimly appropriate than ever. Today one of its principal products is food stamps."

Representative Henry Reuss

The city has never been viewed as a producer of basic wealth. Mining and extraction are considered outside the capacity of urban areas. Even manufacturing is considered to need so much land area and to serve such large markets that it must locate outside cities. The urban community generally is seen as the site of finance, commerce and service industries. The self-reliant city changes this definition. The city becomes a producer of basic wealth and a processor of raw materials as well as a site of commerce and trade.

One of the most important problems will be to identify new sources of energy to heat our buildings, power our machines and fuel our vehicles. Fortunately, the dramatic price increases in fossil fuels during the 1970s spurred the creation of a vibrant industry to serve those interested in reducing energy imports and generating energy on-site. The $100 million energy conservation industry in 1973 had grown to $4 billion by 1979 and to $10 billion by 1982. That put it on a par with total Japanese imported car sales in the United States. *Business Week* predicts gross annual sales will reach $50 billion by 1990, equal to all car sales in the U.S. whether imported or domestically produced. It is an indication of how the times have changed that an industry which was only a bit player in the economy a decade ago has come to play such an essential role, while the automobile industry, a decade ago the centerpiece of our society, has become an economic albatross.

In moving toward an energy efficient community, cities can also rely on new technologies. Infrared cameras can locate building heat losses. Lights are now available that turn themselves off automatically when people leave the room and adjust their intensity levels to the amount of sunlight coming in the windows.

Existing buildings can save up to 80 percent of their energy with investments that repay themselves in fewer than ten years. Refrigerators are now commercially available that use 90 percent less electricity to provide the same cooling space as those in our homes today. Today's automobiles use 250 gallons a year compared to the 1,000 gallons a year used by those purchased a decade before.

Thus, the city seeking self-reliance can reduce its imported energy simply by making its physical stock more efficient. Moreover, new technologies now make it feasible for the city to become an energy producer. For example, buildings can now tap into the warmth of the soil, ground water or air around them. While the ground water may not be warm to the touch, its year round temperature of 50 degrees means that we need only a small amount of external energy to boost it to the 100 to 140 degree range necessary for space or water heating purposes.

Rising prices of natural gas make it desirable to tap into small deposits located under our cities. The Harbor School District in Erie, Pennsylvania, developed two wells between 1978 and 1980. To improve the payback, the school district converted its 34 vehicles, including 25 school buses, to compressed natural gas. The wells paid for themselves in 17 months, and the school district continues to find new cost benefits. The gas burns cleaner than gasoline and the carbon buildup on the engine has almost been eliminated. Tuneups have been extended to once every 24,000 miles rather than 12,000. Oil changes now occur every 6,000 rather than every 2,000 miles. Youngstown, Ohio, uses its natural gas resources in a different manner. It leases land at one of its municipal airports to a private company in return for a percentage of the gross revenue and a priority given to local businesses on gas sales from the land.

Sufficient sunlight falls on most of our city rooftops to heat our buildings. Unfortunately, the sunlight does not fall at precisely the time we need the heat. In some cities, 75 percent of the solar energy falls during the summer, yet 90 percent of the heating needs occur during the winter, when days are shorter and sunlight is less intense. These cities need to develop seasonal storage systems. Our household water tanks store 50 to 75 gallons of water. With only an inch or so of insulation, the water stays hot for 24 hours. Improving on the potential, Sweden and Canada have built immense underground storage tanks that are heavily insulated. Solar collectors convert the sunlight to heat during the summer. The heat is used during the winter months. Six or even nine months storage has proven economical in Sweden, whose latitude is more than 1,000 miles north of Boston, Massachusetts. Miamisburg, Ohio, has used a seasonal storage system called a solar pond to heat a part of one building since 1979.

The ice pond uses the same principles of thermodynamics as the solar pond. Physicist Ted Taylor uses a simple device to spray water into the air in the cold winter months. The water quickly freezes, dropping into an underground tank. During the summer the ice melts, cooling the interior of nearby buildings. Thus, we can store the summer's heat or the winter's cold for use six months later.

Some startling breakthroughs have taken place in electrical generation. Next to the car, the power plant has been the symbol of modern America. Ten pecent of all our primary fuels were burned to generate electricity in 1930, 20 percent in 1960, 30 percent today, and some observers predict the fraction used to generate this high-quality energy source might rise to 50 percent by the year 2000. For a century, the average power plant grew in size. The largest central electric station served 3,000 households in 1900. By 1980, the largest facility under construction would serve 3,000,000 households. As power plants grew larger they also became more remote. In 1982 the average kilowatt hour travelled 220 miles.

The drawback of large power plants is that they take a long time to come on-line. Currently, it takes more than a decade to plan, construct and begin to operate an electric power plant. Such long lead times demand very accurate predictive capability. Between 1880 and 1970, electric demand increased predictably by seven percent a year, doubling every ten years. But after the price hikes of the 1970s, industry began to develop more efficient electric conversion devices and households began to use electricity more wisely. Electric demand is now doubling nationally every 40 years. In some parts of the nation, demand is actually declining. Thus, power plants now coming on-line which were planned in 1973 are no longer needed. Even as the ability to predict far into the future diminishes, rising interest rates and construction cost overruns increase the financial penalty associated with wrong guesses. Billions of dollars were spent on central generating stations which now sit idle. In many parts of the country, utilities have twice as much generating capacity as their customers need during the year. In 1981, the president of the American Public Power Association expressed his hope that none of his organization's 2,200 members would ever again build a large central power station.

Smaller power plants are only one implication of rising energy prices. Another is more efficient power plants. Traditionally, more than 70 percent of the fuel burned in central stations is lost as waste heat. Less than a third is delivered as electricity. Today, more and more companies are building power plants that not only generate electricity but also can capture the waste heat for useful purposes. But since the cost of transporting heat long distances is very high, the best location for these cogeneration facilities is near the customer. Thus, the combination of smaller power plants and cogeneration moves electric generation back into our communities, reversing a century-long trend. A 1978 study for the state of New Jersey concluded that almost 50 percent of the boilers in the state were over 25 years old and would soon require replacement. They could be replaced with devices that are up to 98 percent efficient, that is, that convert 98 percent of the energy value of the fuel source to electricity and heat.

In 1980, the Italian automobile giant, FIAT, carried this dynamic to its logical conclusion by introducing the Total Energy Module System. The

TOTEM system is a converted automobile engine. Heat recovery and noise-reducing casing is attached. The device is no larger than a washing machine and no more noisy than a gas furnace. Using methane, natural gas or oil as a fuel, the TOTEM sells for $15,000 and generates heat and electricity for up to eight houses. The household power plant is almost here.

Rising energy prices not only encourage decentralized power plant locations. They also encourage the use of decentralized fuels. Unlike coal, uranium, petroleum and natural gas, renewable fuels such as sunlight, water, plant matter and wind are located more or less equally around the globe. One community may have less direct sunlight and more rainfall. Another might have more wind and less plant matter. As conventional fuel prices increase, the economic potential for renewables expands exponentially. For example, only gigantic hydroelectric dams were competitive with diesel generators in the 1950s. Dam up the Columbia River and generate power for 200,000 homes. But in the 1970s, rising electric prices made smaller rivers economically exploitable. Suddenly, small-scale hydro facilities serving 20,000 households became competitive with petroleum-driven power plants. By the early 1980s, rising electric prices had introduced a new term to the energy vocabulary—micro hydro. Run-of-the-river devices requiring no dams at all could generate power for fewer than 100 homes and still be competitive. Tens of thousands of backyard streams suddenly took on renewed economic importance. Cities that had been founded 200 years before on the shores of fast flowing rivers for a source of mechanical power began refurbishing their abandoned damsites. Some cities found new sources of water power. La Habra, California, installed a 100-kilowatt turbine in its water pipes.

Recognizing the need to encourage decentralized and efficient power plants, the federal government in 1978 enacted the Public Utility Regulatory Policy Act. That Act abolished the century-old monopoly utilities held over power production. From March 1981 onwards, utilities have had to purchase independently produced power at premium prices. They must allow independent producers to interconnect with the grid system and must not place any undue burden on these producers. Although utilities have often only reluctantly agreed to the tenets of this new law, and lawsuits blossomed immediately against the authority of the federal government to enact such legislation, there is no mistaking the tenor of these times. The grid system has become a giant, guaranteed market.

The most exciting technology for on-site electric generation is a device developed for space use. The photovoltaic or solar cell converts direct sunlight into electricity. Until 1974, its only use was to power satellites. In 1974, one could outfit a residence for $2 million. By 1982, the price was $45,000 for household self-sufficiency, still too high for most households, but a 50-fold reduction in price in eight years. More than 500 homes already are equipped with solar cells. Many of these homes are located away from power lines. The cost of laying cable to the homes is greater than the cost of purchasing the solar devices and backup systems or battery storage systems. By 1985, industry and government experts agree these devices will be widespread in the residential and commercial sectors. Indeed, this technology is cost-effective at the household level first. Only as the price drops further does it become competitive for use in central locations. The reason for this apparent anomaly is that central facilities require large investments in land and arrays upon which to place the solar cells. Also, there is a ten percent loss of electricity in transmitting from a central facility.

General Electric, the company formed when Thomas Edison left the power plant business in the late 1880s, developed in prototype form a rooftop solar cell shingle in 1982. Not available yet commercially, these shingles will transform the roof into a power plant. GE eyes the two million homes that are re-roofed each year as its potential market.

What happens when rooftops become power plants? A housing development in Phoenix has a home equipped with 1,000 square feet of rooftop solar cells. This house generates more electricity than is needed by the occupants on a year-round basis. The developer, John Long, includes in the purchase price of the house the buyer's choice of one of three models of electric vehicles. When the rooftop becomes a power plant, the car becomes a household appliance.

One thousand square feet of solar cells generate electricity worth $750 to $1,000 at today's prices. A rough rule of thumb in the real estate industry is that the gross sales value of a house is ten times its rental income. Thus, the value of a house equipped with solar cells will be increased by $10,000. A house on the north side of the street facing due south may be worth considerably more than one on the south side of the street facing due north. When photovoltaics enter our cities, the very land values of our neighborhoods will change.

In 1920, 4,000 power plants served the nation. In 1980, the same number did so. By 1990, as many as one million power plants will be in operation and by the year 2000 more than four million. These will be tiny plants. But they will represent a considerable political constituency. One of the major tasks of cities will be to develop institutional mechanisms to integrate these new technologies into existing structures.

Solar storage units, rooftop collectors, and another form of solar energy—food production, will require considerable space. The prevailing image of the American city is of congestion. Manhattan, with a density of 140 people per acre, serves as the classic example of urban areas. However, the average city of more than 100,000 people has a density of fewer than seven people per acre, closer to that of Staten Island than Manhattan. The density of Oklahoma City, which has fewer than one person per acre, is closer to the national average for our fastest growing cities (those with populations of 25,000 to 50,000) than is Manhattan. As Daniel Eleazar wrote ten years ago, "many of these American-style city dwellers—in every socioeconomic bracket—actually live on plots of land that would look large to a Chinese or Indian farmer."[26] One study done in the early 1970s found that among a sample of 86 cities with populations over 100,000, the average amount of vacant land available per capita was 2,279 square feet.[27] This ranged from a high of 6,279 square feet in the West South Central states, to 360 square feet in the Mid-Atlantic region. Of this sample, it was found that Beaumont had 68 percent of its land vacant, and about half of San Diego and Phoenix at that time consisted of vacant land. Another study involving 38 cities in Oregon found that those with populations between 10,000 and 50,000 had about 30 percent of their land area vacant.[28] This enormous land reserve could be available for agriculture. Current American per capita annual consumption of food requires about an acre of land. According to one study:[29]

> a conservative estimate of the numbers of people that can be fed on a vegetarian diet with or without dairy products is about four per acre ... This figure does not include lengthening the growing season with greenhouses. A diet including fish or meat two or three times a week would increase the amount of land needed by at least 25 to 50 percent.

John Jeavons and Michael Shepard determined, on the basis of three years' growing experience, that a full, balanced diet may eventually be grown on as little as 2,500 square feet per person in a six-month growing season.[30]

W. Jackson Davis took the data which formed the basis for the study of 86 cities noted above, and estimated the amount of open space in the cities on which food could, in principle, be grown.[32] He then chose as his benchmark the highly efficient, non-industrial agriculture of the Chinese, in which about 18 persons per acre can gain subsistence diets. He found that the percentage of subsistence level diets that could be reached ranges from 16 percent in Detroit to almost 60 percent in New York City.

The federal Department of Agriculture counts a property as a farm if the tenant earns $1,000 in agriculture-related income from it. Such earnings would be easily achievable by high-yield gardening in most of our cities.

To grow food, we need adequate water and fertilizers. The city is a giant nutrient machine, spewing out organic and human wastes. These can be used as fertilizers. In fact, municipal composting operations are increasingly commonplace around the country. One study of the Omaha-Council Bluffs area in Nebraska found that from sludge alone "more nutrients are available . . . than the average supplied by Nebraska farmers." It concludes, "By the year 2000, with increasing waste volume and rising fertilizer prices, benefits to the region's farmers in terms of supplying crop nutrients could exceed $1 million annually."[32] Another report concluded that the combined nitrogen disposed of by municipalities in America is greater than the total amount used in nitrogen fertilizers in the early 1970s.

It is quite possible that cities would want to use the land surrounding the city as a giant greenbelt, much as Davis, California, and a number of other cities are planning. Given cooperation among metropolitan authorities, or annexation power by the municipality, the land area involved and, therefore, production potential could be greatly extended.

In 1949, Egon Glesinger, in his classic, *The Coming Age of Wood*, forcefully argued for an industrial civilization based on wood.[33] Noting that an acre of forest could yield annually several times as much fiber as cotton, and as much sugar as the same soil planted in sugar beets, he concluded,

> It can be readily demonstrated that the renewable biomass on our planet is quantitatively sufficient to supply the needs of the current world populations. It can also be shown that we possess the needed chemical technology for the production from biomass of many of the commodities that we now produce from fossil fuels, such as fuel oil, gasoline, and synthetic polymers.

Timber yields have greatly increased since 1949. Presently, the new annual growth of U.S. forests is 38 cubic feet per acre per year. The average American uses about 75 cubic feet of wood products for all purposes. Thus, two acres would be required to supply the wood needs of an average American.[34,35]

However, the major portion of wood products, outside structural and veneer uses, is for packaging, and most of this packaging is unnecessary. Paper made from wood is easily recycled. We might see our consumption of wood being reduced for these uses as the wood supply expands to become a source of pharmaceuticals or synthetics.

It is possible, however, to use the woody plants instead of timber. Just before World War I, the Department of Agriculture investigated advantages of hemp, which had been a source of paper before the chemical pulping process was introduced in the middle of the nineteenth century. The study concluded that hemp could produce four times the pulp per acre as wood, that paper made from it lasted much longer, and that it had the unique advantage of growing to maturation in a single season. The tragedy of forest fires that wipe out 40 years of growth would be minimized.

There are now bagasse factories, bamboo factories, straw factories. One of the most promising plants appears to be kenaf, which yields 3.7 to 12.4 tons per acre, some five to eight times more than wood. Thus, it appears that one could reduce the current land area required per American to about one half acre per person, making it conceivable that a city greenbelt could produce almost all the raw materials necessary for our industrial civilization.[36]

What other resources are available to the city? A city the size of Dayton has more than 50,000 students in its public school system. If the city has a city university or a community college, there may be several thousand more. It has thousands of teachers with a wide range of skills. It has laboratory space, computers, and machine tool shops through its vocational training centers. We treat our students as consumers of knowledge during their tenure in our educational system, rather than as producers of wealth. A student can learn trigonometry while sizing a solar collector as well as by doing abstract exercises in the back of a textbook. A student can learn chemistry by analyzing soil to be used to raise vegetables, or by analyzing the nutritional content of those vegetables, as well as he or she can by doing lab exercises. The ancient aphorism, "I hear and I forget. I see and I remember. I do and I understand," still holds true. Our schools should be able to contribute greatly to our community. One school system in Hazen, North Dakota, grinds its own wheat, and buys its own beef from local rangers and dairy producers. "Why should we only be turning out welders?" Superintendent Joe Crawford asks, "Why not meat cutters?" In late 1978, Hazen became the only school in North Dakota to get a federal custom permit to operate an inspected meat plant. The next step is to become a fully licensed custom meat plant so students can sell meat to other schools and customers. Students also process whole frozen chickens.

In Hartford, Connecticut, the "workplace" program links up school systems to local businesses. Students earn money while working in businesses in fields that they are studying in school. Hartford has gone one step further, setting up an auto mechanic business where students earn while they learn, providing a top quality service to the community while gaining credit toward a degree that will help them in later life.

Cities have the resource base to move toward local self-reliance. Not self-sufficiency, but independence—looking inward instead of outward, building on their scientific and technical knowledge to design systems that maximize the benefit to the city as a whole.

As cities look to retain as much economic value within their borders as possible, they will inevitably turn their attention toward manufacturing and processing. We are taught that large is best, that the model is the automobile assembly lines in Detroit, or the Gary, Indiana, steel mills. As we have had to reconceptualize our cities to see them as mines or power plants, so we must change our thinking about the scale required for efficient manufacturing. The self-reliant city can increasingly make it at home.

The City as Factory: Making It at Home

"City: a settlement that consistently generates its economic growth from its own local economy."

Jane Jacobs

Harvard economist Joe Bain, in a classic study of economies of scale in manufacturing, concluded, "... after a century and a half of rapid industrial expansion, of extraordinary technical progress, and of generalized belief in the virtues of size, it still remains that the average factory in the United States or Great Britian employs only two or three score people . . ."[37]

Researchers have since come to a similar conclusion—most of the things we need could be manufactured within our larger urban areas. One study found that, if automobiles and petroleum products were excluded from the total, 58 percent of final goods consumption, by value, of a population of one million could be produced locally in small plants. Sixteen percent of the consumption needs could be produced by plants for a market population of 200,000.[38] Even very small factories raised production costs only slightly.[39] A shoe factory which produces for a city of 100,000, instead of a region of 500,000, may have production costs only five to ten percent higher. Since production costs only represent a small fraction of the selling price, such increases could be offset by eliminating middleman profits or reducing transportation expenses. Cities could, through their taxing or procurement policies, value locally produced items higher than those which are imported.

Most of these studies of plant sizes look at existing technologies. Economist John Blair, described a more recent phenomenon, the rise of what he dubs "centrifugal technologies."[40]

> With plastics, fiberglass, and high performance composites providing high strength and easily processed materials suitable for

an infinite variety of applications; with energy provided by such simple and efficient devices as high energy batteries, fuel cells, turbine engines, and rotary piston engines; with computers providing a means of instantaneously retrieving, sorting and aggregating vast bodies of information; and with other new electronic devices harnessing the flow of electrons for other uses, there appears to be aborning a second industrial revolution which, among its other features, contains within itself the seeds of destruction for concentrated industrial structures.

For example, in the late 1960s one plastics executive said: "A thermoforming mold made of epoxy costs approximately one to two percent of an equivalent steel stamping die, and we have yet to find out how many pieces can be run from a mold." Plastic-bodied cars can be produced at much less cost than steel-bodied vehicles. One observer notes, "The outside availability of power train components and the use of plastic bodies should reduce his capital costs markedly below what is currently required to enter the industry at any given level of output."[41] The close tolerances required of piston engines are not necessary for electric vehicles, reducing the need for both capital and labor. One British car manufacturer described the electric car as a "far less complex vehicle than the existing motor car and contains about one-fifth of the parts that are in present-day cars." The tooling required to produce a plastic-bodied car in the late 1960s was about $1.5 million, compared to the $500 million then required to initiate production of conventional steel-bodied piston engine cars.

Internal combustion engine, steel-bodied car factories are economical only if they sell more than 150,000 vehicles a year. Conventional electric vehicle factories need sell only 7,000 medium-priced cars to financially survive. One enterprising Italian manufacturer has developed production techniques that can manufacture as few as 500 electric vehicles a year and still generate a profit.

In Nebraska, a problem—what to do with millions of car and truck tires—generated a new technology. The increased use of steel-belted radials makes it uneconomical to use conventional mechanical shredding processes for tires. But new techniques use liquid nitrogen to freeze the tire to hundreds of degrees below zero. The rubber is then pulverized. The steel and fiber is also captured. The powdered crumb rubber is then converted into a wide variety of products, from rubber soles to floorboard or road surfacing agents. Modern science again has taken a disposal problem and made it into a production process.

Hercules, California, a city of 7,000, wanted to grow, but the Environmental Protection Agency prohibited growth without a commitment to expensive new sewage treatment capacity. Bypassing federal strictures, the city chose to build a sewage plant called Aquacell with its own money. The system consists of an inflated polyethylene greenhouse cover built over three treatment lagoons. Duckweed and water hyacinths grow on the pond's surface, existing on nutrients in the waste water and screening out the sun to inhibit algae growth. The plants can be harvested or can be composted by themselves or along with the sludge to produce fertilizer. Harvested alone, the plants, high in protein, can become animal feed. Methane is generated during the digestion process, and can be used to fulfill some of the electrical requirements of the plant. The system can be built in modular form. Once again, modern science has created an elegant, integrated system that transforms a waste facility into a production plant.

The idea that there might be a variety of capital and labor tradeoffs in manufacturing was proven most dramatically by Ernst Schumacher and his London-based organization, the Intermediate Technology Development Group. In 1972 while visiting Zambia at the invitation of the president, he discovered a serious economic crisis; the farmers could not get their eggs to market because of a labor strike at the egg carton factory. Schumacher was surprised to learn that the factory was in the Netherlands. After returning to Europe he sought out the president of the company, and asked him whether it might be feasible to design a factory to meet only the needs of the small market of Zambia, which required but one million egg cartons a year. The president, speaking from 30-years' experience, answered that his factory was designed to be more efficient, and that if any factory were to produce egg cartons at less than the rate of one million a month it would have to produce them at a higher cost.

Undaunted, Schumacher set his team to work. Eighteen months later an egg carton manufacturing plant was operational in Zambia. It produced, not one million egg cartons a year, but only a third of a million, for there were three distinct egg market areas in the country, and three factories were needed. The plants produced egg cartons at the same unit costs, were more labor intensive, and used local materials. When industrial engineers were asked why they never designed a factory like that before, their answer was "Because no one asked us to."

In Chile, a colleague of Schumacher was asked if he could find a supplier of glass jam jars to replace those imported from Britain. The researcher recalled, "The mind boggles at the thought of a boatload of empty jam jars being transported there to be filled with jam, and then exported back again to the Western World. I thought that was basically crazy." He found that glass was made primarily from sand, limestone, soda ash, and a few trace elements like arsenic. Soda ash could be replaced with seaweed, but the glass would be slightly green. Arsenic could be eliminated, but there would be tiny bubbles in the glass. A furnace normally cost about 25,000 English pounds because it required highly sophisticated refractory materials. The reason why these materials were used was that the furnace was expected to last for 10 years. But if there were local refractory clay, and the people were prepared to reline every six months with refractory bricks, the proposed plant could produce one thousand jars an hour with local raw products for a modest investment.

This last example holds important lessons. Local self-reliance may require tradeoffs. A functionally equivalent product may be manufactured in a variety of ways, depending on how much the producer wants to substitute indigenous resources for imported resources.

Localism and Globalism

Local self-reliance is a positive concept. It implies strengthening the local economy, and building self-confidence and skills at the local level. But it can also imply parochialism and rivalry.

One may wonder how much more parochial and competitive we can be, with cities fighting with cities to attract scarce corporations, to be awarded scarce federal contracts, to be allocated scarce petroleum. Cities are stealing about anything they can from their neighbors, including sports teams.

Parochialism can be combatted only by a massive dose of information. Currently the mass media tell us what the corporate and national leadership are doing, thinking and wearing. But the real news—stories about cities with problems similar to ours, or small businesses with similar products, or neighborhoods with similar situations—seldom make it even to human interest spots on network news. Striving for local self-reliance can provide a basis for a dramatic increase in city-to-city and neighborhood-to-neighborhood information exchange. With over 10,000 cities and counties, such an exchange could effect a significant transfer of innovations.

Another problem of local self-reliance is the potential that it will slip into what our British friends call "local selfish-sufficiency." America is enormously rich in money, technology and natural resources. For most of the world, our crises would be luxuries. A gasoline line would be envied by most of the world, where dung or increasingly scarce wood, are their only fuels and a donkey provides their transportation.

Yet our search for local self-reliance can help us develop and share information relevant to other nations. As we learn to design our cities to live within their resource budget, we will be developing systems that can teach and learn from those in other nations. City-to-city exchanges in this country might be one byproduct of local self-reliance. Exchanges on an international level might be another result.

Aiding this horizontal flow of information are the extraordinary developments in communications and electronics. We can have a global electronic village as we develop a globe of materially self-reliant villages.

The growth of the electronics, computer and communications industries is based on the ability to get more productivity out of fewer raw materials. The objective is to store more information on a given area. Every two years the semiconductor industry quadruples the amount of memory that can be stored for the same price.

We can now ship vastly greater quantities of electrons from one part of the globe to another using much less energy. "The road upon which our electronic freight travels is the electromagnetic spectrum. The way we have broadened the use of this spectrum is comparable to going from country dirt roads to the major interstate highways. But while automobiles have become more and more resource-consuming over the years, taking up more and more of the road, the advances in electronic transmission

Municipal Democracy

	Recall	Initiative	Referendum	Direct Democracy Index
HIGH:				
Hawaii (1)*	100%	100%	100%	100%
Alaska (17)	94%	94%	100%	96%
Colorado (63)	97%	89%	98%	95%
Oregon (71)	92%	96%	97%	95%
South Dakota (14)	100%	85%	100%	95%
Arizona (41)	98%	90%	93%	94%
California (326)	96%	90%	93%	93%
Michigan (197)	96%	83%	95%	91%
Ohio (188)	87%	87%	93%	89%
Montana (20)	85%	83%	88%	85%
Florida (159)	89%	66%	93%	83%
North Dakota (9)	86%	80%	78%	81%
Nevada (10)	91%	67%	80%	79%
Nebraska (35)	74%	72%	88%	78%
Oklahoma (78)	89%	60%	84%	78%
Idaho (18)	84%	72%	71%	76%
Arkansas (30)	71%	63%	78%	71%
Texas (240)	78%	59%	77%	71%
New Jersey (182)	68%	62%	79%	70%
Kansas (69)	76%	55%	77%	69%
Wisconsin (105)	76%	48%	78%	67%

One way to determine the democratic nature of cities is the extent to which they permit citizens to directly participate in the governing process. Recall is the ability to remove a local elected official before the end of his or her term. Initiative is the ability to directly initiate and enact legislation. Referendum is the ability to vote on legislation enacted by the elected city government.

This chart lists the percent of cities that permit each type of direct participation. A crude democracy index shows the average fraction of all cities that have all these forms of direct participation. Those in the highest category have a democracy index above 66%. Those in the medium category have an index between 66% and 33%. Those in the lowest category have a democracy index below 33%.

Municipal Democracy

	Recall	Initiative	Referendum	Direct Democracy Index
MEDIUM:				
Washington (62)	91%	51%	52%	65%
Maine (112)	29%	76%	80%	62%
New Hampshire (47)	36%	74%	76%	62%
Louisiana (43)	90%	27%	63%	60%
Connecticut (94)	31%	53%	87%	57%
Massachusetts (137)	34%	72%	65%	57%
South Carolina (58)	40%	55%	75%	57%
Vermont (32)	20%	67%	84%	57%
West Virginia (38)	47%	40%	85%	57%
Minnesota (128)	47%	50%	72%	56%
Mississippi (29)	52%	31%	73%	52%
Maryland (35)	15%	42%	92%	50%
Rhode Island (19)	17%	41%	91%	50%
Missouri (100)	55%	37%	55%	49%
Pennsylvania (209)	27%	27%	89%	48%
Illinois (219)	30%	33%	71%	45%
New Mexico (25)	48%	22%	48%	39%
New York (134)	16%	21%	79%	39%
Utah (30)	22%	36%	59%	39%
Delaware (9)	0%	44%	67%	37%
Tennessee (78)	35%	14%	62%	37%
Iowa (77)	28%	30%	51%	36%
Georgia (84)	44%	14%	46%	35%
Wyoming (10)	47%	19%	33%	33%
LOW:				
North Carolina (101)	24%	20%	53%	32%
Alabama (43)	33%	15%	36%	28%
Kentucky (41)	21%	20%	33%	25%
Virginia (66)	13%	89%	51%	24%
Indiana (66)	14%	6%	36%	19%

*Number of cities reporting in each state represents, on average, more than 90 percent of all cities in state.
Source: *The Municipal Year Book, 1979*, International City Management Association, Washington, D.C., page 111-143, (original table contains data on 4,870 municipalities).

have allowed us to use less and less of a lane to accomplish the same purpose, and allowed us to continue to open more lanes of this natural highway."[42]

That we could exhaust the potential of the electromagnetic spectrum appears unlikely—it is a constantly renewable highway for transporting information. This aspect of the nature of the resource is crucial, because an energy-efficient society is a knowledge-intensive society.

The discovery that the electromagnetic spectrum is a major source of wealth comes at a propitious time for municipalities; they have the authority to issue franchises for cable television. A century ago, cities learned of the value of the electricity franchise and slowly gained an ability to design franchises that enhanced the public welfare. The communication franchise is more complex but amenable to the same process. Already about three dozen municipalities have decided to own their own electronic highways. Conway, Arkansas, a town of 20,000 will not only provide entertainment over its channels, but fire and burglar alarms, load management for the municipally owned electric system, banking and meter reading. It estimates that over a 15-year period the municipally owned system will generate almost $10,000 a year more in city revenues than if it were privately owned.

Other cities, like Davis and St. Paul are seriously examining the potential of consumer-owned cable systems. Neither the municipal corporation nor outside investors will own the information highways of the future. Rather, the actual users of the systems will be its owners.

The controversy over cable T.V. and the role of the city in its regulation and ownership is only another of the many resource issues that characterize our era.

There will be hard choices involved in deciding what we will do with our resources. Questions of equity, scale and environment will arise; yet that, above all, is the role of the political process. Politics only recently has been a process by which we vote for people. Originally, it was a process by which we actively participated in allocating resources. Hundreds of cities still allow their citizens to make decisions directly. As Alexis de Tocqueville wrote, "Town meetings are to liberty what primary schools are to science. They bring it within the people's reach. A nation may establish a free government, but without municipal institutions it cannot have the spirit of liberty."

And, of course, there is the problem of confronting those centralizing forces that are so powerful today. The 1980s will be a period of social turmoil. Those who want to use local self-reliance as an excuse to drop out of society will find it impossible. Although local self-reliance, recycling, small-scale production, solar energy and preventive rather than treatment systems may make more sense, we have to confront and transform institutions built in another era, when resources were plentiful, growth was the objective, and affluence was a never-ending spiral. We are cursed with giant central power plants, interlocking directorates between big corporations, big factories, and big government, production systems far removed from their markets, bloated bureaucracies which are on the whole unproductive, if not downright destructive, and hierarchical organizational structures which remove the top policymakers from the impact of their decisions. We are cursed but not condemned.

We are at a turning point in history. The opportunity exists to marry local political authority to the advantages of modern technology to make more independent self-reliant communities. Only at the local level can we design humanly scaled production systems that meet our unique local requirements. We can seize the opportunity and potential that comes from a period of rapid social change, and design a society in which we, and our children, would want to live. So far, to be sure, the positive signs are few. Yet they point the way to a new vision, a new context, . . . and a new way of thinking.

References

1. Kropotkin, Petr, *Mutual Aid*, (Boston: Extending Horizon Books, 1955), pp. 162-163.
2. Ibid., p. 200.
3. Goodman, W. I. and Freund, E. C., *Principles and Practices of Urban Planning*, (Washington, D.C.: ICMA, 1968), p. 13.
4. Ibid.
5. Ibid., p. 16.
6. Weber, Adna, *The Growth of Cities in the Nineteenth Century*, (New York: Columbia Univ. Press, 1963).
7. "City of Clinton vs. The Cedar Rapids and Missouri River Railroad," 24 *Iowa Law Review* 455 (1868).
8. Hunter vs. Pittsburgh, 207 United States 161, 178 (1907).
9. Goodman and Freund, *Urban Planning*, pg. 23.
10. Ibid.
11. Nolen, John, *New Ideals in the Planning of Cities, Towns, and Villages*, (Boston: Marshall Jones Company, 1927), pp. 133-134.
12. Goodman and Freund, *Urban Planning*, p. 26.
13. Shannon, John and Ross, John, "Cities: Their Increasing Dependence on State and Federal Aid," in Harrington J. Bryce, *Small Cities in Transition: The Dynamics of Growth and Decline*, (Cambridge: Ballinger Publishing Co., 1977), p. 189.
14. Carswell, Elizabeth, *Less is More*, (Madison, Wis., 1974).
15. Pierce, Neil, "Smokestack Chasers Who Miss the Point," *Washington Post*, 30 May 1977.
16. *Business Week*, 21 June 1976.
17. *Wall Street Journal*, 22 March 1978.
18. Mueller, Charles, testifying in hearings on "The Future of Small Business in America," Report to the Committee on Antitrust, Consumers and Employment of the Committee on Small Business, U.S. House of Representatives 95th Congress, 1978.
19. Stein, Barry and Hodax, Mark, *Competitive Scale in Manufacturing: The Case of Consumer Goods*, (Cambridge: Center for Community Economic Development, 1977).
20. Representative Morris Udall, *National Journal*, 30 July 1977.
21. Rifkin, Jeremy and Howard, Ted, *Who Shall Play God?* (New York: Dell Publishing Co., 1977), p. 105.
22. Birch, David, *The Job Generation Process*, (Cambridge, MIT Press, 1979).
23. City of St. Paul vs. Dalfin, Minnesota.
24. 89 Cal Rpts at 905, citing Miller vs. Board of Public Works, 234 p. 2d 381 at 383.

25. Central Lumber Co. vs. Waseca 1922, 152 Minn 201, 1888.

26. Eleazar, Daniel, "Are We a Nation of Cities?" *The Public Interest*, No. 4 (1965-66), p. 95.

27. Northern, Ray M., *Vacant Urban Land in the American City*, (Corvalis: Oregon State University, 1971).

28. Bureau of Municipal Research and Service, Planning Bulletin no. 2, (Eugene: University of Oregon, 1961).

29. Connor, Michael, staff paper, Washington, D.C. Institute for Local Self-Reliance, 1975.

30. Jeavons, John, 1972-1975 Research Report Summary on the Biodynamic French Intensive Method, (Palo Alto: *Ecology Action*, 1976).

31. Davis, W. Jackson, *The Seventh Year: Industrial Civilization in Transition*, (New York: W. W. Norton & Co., 1979), p. 232, citing C. Abrams, "The Uses of Land in Cities," *Scientific American*, 213 (1965): 150-162.

32. Blobaum, Roger, *The Use of Sewage and Solid Wastes in Metropolitan Omaha*, (Washington, D.C.: Roger Blobaum and Associates, 1979).

33. Glesinger, Egon, *The Coming Age of Wood*, (New York: Simon & Schuster, 1949).

34. Spurr, Stephen A. and Vaux, Henry J., "Timber: Biological and Economic Potential," *Science*, 20 February 1976.

35. *Statistical Abstract of the United States*, 1976, "Per Capita Consumption of Timber Products," 1950-1975, p. 681.

36. Atchison, Joseph E., "Agricultural Residues and Other Nonwood Plant Fibers, *Science* 20 February 1975.

37. Bain, Joe S., *Barriers to New Competition*, (Cambridge: Harvard Univ. Press, 1956).

38. Stein, and Hodax, op. cit.

39. See, for example, Scherer, F.M., "Economies of Scale and Industrial Concentration," in Harvey J. Goldschmid, H. Michael Mann, J. Fred Weston (editors), *Industrial Concentration: The New Learning*, (Boston: Little, Brown & Co., 1974).

40. Blair, John, *Economic Concentration*, (New York: Harcourt Brace Jovanovich, 1972), p. 151.

41. Data taken from hearings on Economic Concentration, part 5, Subcommittee on Antitrust and Monopoly, 1967.

42. Morris, David, *Self-Reliant Cities*: Energy and the Transformation of Urban America, (San Francisco: Sierra Club Press, 1982), p. 214.

Selected Bibliography

Alcaly, Roger E. and Marmelstein, David, ed., *The Fiscal Crisis of American Cities,* New York: Vintage Books/Random House, 1976.

Alternatives to Traditional Public Safety Delivery Systems—Municipal Fire Insurance, Berkeley, California: Institute for Local Self Government, 1977.

Anderson, Russell, E., *Biological Paths to Self-Reliance: A Guide to Biological Solar Energy Conversion,* New York: Van Nostrand Réinhold, 1979.

Antieau, Chester, J., *Local Government Law,* Washington, D.C.: Georgetown Univ. Law Center, 1974.

Bach, Eve, et. al., *The Cities' Wealth,* Oakland: Community Ownership Organizing Project 1976.

Baker, Paula, C., Ostrom, Elinor and Goehlert, Robert, *Metropolitan Reform: An Annotated Bibliography,* Bloomington, Indiana: Indiana University, 1979.

Berry, Wendell, *The Unsettling of America:* New York: Avon Books, 1978.

Blair, John, *Economic Concentration,* New York: Harcourt Brace Jovanovich, 1972.

Block, A. Harvey, *Impact Analysis and Local Area Planning: An Input/Output Study,* Cambridge: Center for Community Economic Development, 1977.

Bookchin, Murray, *The Limits of the City,* New York: Harper and Row, 1974.

Bosselman, Fred, Callies, David and Banta, John, *The Taking Issue,* Washington, D.C.: Government Printing Office, 1973.

Bosselman, Fred, Feurer, Duane A. and Siemon, Charles L., *The Permit Explosion: Coordination of the Proliferation,* Washington, D.C.: The Urban Land Institute, 1976.

Bradley, Richard C., *The Costs of Urban Growth: Observations and Judgements,* Colorado Springs: Pikes Peak Area Council of Governments, 1973.

Braverman, Harry, *Labor and Monopoly Capital,* New York: Monthly Review Press, 1974.

Bryce, Herrington J., ed., *Small Cities in Transition: The Dynamics of Growth and Decline,* Cambridge, Mass.: Ballinger Publishing Company, 1977.

Burchell, Robert W. and Listokin, David, *The Fiscal Impact Handbook: Estimating Local Costs and Revenues of Land Development,* New Brunswick: Center for Urban Policy Research, 1978.

Burns, Scott, *Home Inc.,* Garden City, N.Y.: Doubleday & Co., 1975.

Carlson, Richard J., *The End of Medicine,* New York: Wiley Interscience, 1975.

Cassidy, Robert, *Livable Cities,* 1981.

Choate, Pat and Walter, Susan, *America in Ruins: Beyond the Public Works Pork Barrel.* Washington, D.C.: Council of State Planning Agencies, 1981.

Conley, Gary N., "*How to Attract Private Investments into the Inner City Through the Use of Development Subsidies,*" Washington, D.C.: National Council for Urban Economic Development, 1977.

Corbett, Michael, *A Better Place to Live,* Emmaus: Rodale Press, 1981.

De Tocqueville, Alexis, *Democracy in America*, New York: Washington Square Press, 1968.
Economic Practices Manual, Sacramento: Office of Planning and Research, 1978.
Energy Self-Sufficiency in Northampton, Massachusetts, prepared by Hampshire College, Amherst, Massachusetts for the U.S. Department of Energy, Assistant Secretary for Policy and Evaluation, DOE/PE/4706, October 1979.
[The] Federal Role in the Federal System: The Dynamics of Growth: The Condition of Contemporary Federalism: Conflicting Theories and Collapsing Constraints, Washington, D.C.: Advisory Commission of Intergovernmental Relations, August, 1981.
Fink, Stanley, et. al., *Municipal Insurance Pools: An Appropriate Alternative for Local Governments?* Albany: New York State Legislature, Assembly Ways and Means Committee, January 1980.
Fox, Kenneth, *Better City Government*, Philadelphia: Temple Univ. Press, 1977.
Friend, Gil, *Closing the Circle: Management, Nutrient Cycles and Regional Food Systems*, Washington, D.C.: Institute for Local Self-Reliance, 1978.
Galambos, Eva C., *Making Sense Out of Dollars: Economic Analysis for Local Government*, Washington, D.C.: National League of Cities, 1978.
Gartner, Alan and Riessman, Frank, *Self-Help in the Human Services*, San Francisco: Jossey-Bass Publishers, 1977.
Gelfand, Mark I., *A Nation of Cities: The Federal Government and Urban America, 1933-1965*, New York: Oxford University Press, 1975.
Glaeser, Martin G., *Public Utilities in American Capitalism*, New York: The MacMillan Company, 1957.
Gleason, Jack, *The Economics and Feasibility of City-Scale Energy Systems* (The Prospects for District Heating), unpublished, 1982.
Goetze, Rolf, *Neighborhood Monitoring and Analysis: A New Way of Looking at Urban Neighborhoods and How They Change*, Washington, D.C.: U.S. Department of Housing and Urban Development, Office of Policy Development and Research, 1980.
Goldschmid, Harvey J., et. al. (ed.), *Industrial Concentration: The New Learning*, Boston: Little, Brown & Co., 1974.
Goldstein, Benjamin and Davis, Ross, *Neighborhoods in the Urban Economy*, Lexington, Massachusetts: Lexington Books, 1977.
Goodman, W.I. and Freund, E.C., *Principles and Practices in Urban Planning*, Washington, D.C.: International City Management Association 1968.
Grossman, David A., *The Future of New York City's Capital Stock*, Washington, D.C: The Urban Institute, 1979.
Hartshorn, Truman A., *Interpreting the City: An Urban Geography*, New York: John Wiley and Sons, 1980.
Harvey, David, *Society, the City and the Space: Economics of Urbanism*, Washington, D.C.: Association of American Geographers, 1972.
Henderson, Hazel, *Creating Alternative Futures: The End of Economics*, New York: Berkley Publishing Corp., 1978.

Hill, Melvin B., *State Laws Governing Local Government Structure and Administration*, Atlanta: Institute of Government, Univ. of Georgia, 1978.

Hinds, Dudley, Carn, Neil G. and Ordway, Nicholas, *Winning at Zoning*, New York: McGraw-Hill Book Co., 1979.

Hubbell, L. Kenneth (ed.), *Fiscal Crisis in American Cities: The Federal Response*, Cambridge: Ballinger Publishing Col., 1979.

Humphrey, Nancy, Peterson, George E. and Wilson, Peter, *The Future of Cleveland's Capital Plant*, Washington, D.C.: The Urban Institute, 1979.

[The] *Integral Urban House: Self-Reliant Living in the City*, San Francisco: Sierra Club Books, 1979.

Jacobs, Jane, *The Economy of Cities*, New York: Vintage, 1970.

Jequier, Nicholas, *Appropriate Technology: Problems and Promises*, Paris: Organization for Economic Cooperation and Development, 1976.

Kaplan, Samuel, *The Dream Deferred*, New York: Vintage Books/Random House, 1977.

Kirschner, Edward M. and Morey, James L., *Community Ownership in New Towns and Old Cities*, Cambridge: Center for Community Economic Development, 1975.

Kohr, Leopold, *The Breakdown of Nations*, New York: E.P. Dutton, 1978.

Kohr, Leopold, *The City of Man* (The Duke of Buen Consejo), Puerto Rico: Editorial Universitaria, Universidad de Puerto Rico, 1976.

Kotler, Milton, *The Disappearance of Municipal Liberty*, Washington, D.C.: Institute for Policy Studies, 1970.

Kotler, Milton, *Neighborhood Government*, New York: Bobbs-Merrill Co., 1970.

Kropotkin, Petr, *Mutual Aid*, Boston: Extending Horizons Book, 1955.

Lamb, Robert and Rappaport, Stephen P., Municipal Bonds: *The Comprehensive Review of Tax-Exempt Securities and Public Finance*, New York: Mc-Graw-Hill Book Company, 1980.

Lett, Monica R., *Rent Control: Concepts, Realities and Mechanisms*, New Brunswick, New Jersey: Center for Urban Policy Research, 1976.

Long, Norton, *The Unwalled City: Reconstituting the Urban Community*, New York: Basic Books, 1972.

Lovell, Catherine, et. al., *Federal and State Mandating on Local Governments and Exploration of Impacts and Issues*, Riverside, Ca.: Graduate School of Administration, Univ. of California, 1979.

Lovins, Amory, B., *Soft Energy Paths*, New York: Harper & Row, 1979.

Marciniak, Ed, *Reversing Urban Decline*, Washington, D.C.: National Center for Urban Ethnic Affairs, 1981.

Martines, Lauro, *Power and Imagination: City-States in Renaissance Italy*, New York: Alfred A. Knopf, 1979.

Materials and Man's Needs, Washington, D.C.: National Academy of Sciences, 1975.

McKelvey, Blake, *The Urbanization of America*, New Brunswick, New Jersey: Rutgers University Press, 1916.

Merrill, Richard, ed., *Radical Agriculture*, New York: Harper Colophon Edition, 1976.

Messing, Marc, Friesema, H. Paul and Morell, David, *Centralized Power: The Politics of Scale in Electricity Generation*, Cambridge: Oelgeschlager, Gunn and Hain, Publishers, Inc., 1979.
Metsner, Arnold, J., *The Politics of City Planning*, Berkeley: Univ. of California Press, 1974.
Morris, Charles R., *The Cost of Good Intentions: New York City and the Liberal Experiment 1960-1975*, New York: W.W. Norton and Company, 1980.
Morris, David, *Planning for Energy Self-Reliance: A Case Study of the District of Columbia*, Washington, D.C.: Institute for Local Self-Reliance, 1979.
Morris, David and Hess, Karl, *Neighborhood Power: The New Localism*, Boston: Beacon Press, 1975.
Morris, David, *Self-Reliant Cities: Energy and the Transformation of Urban America*, San Francisco: Sierra Club Books, 1982.
Morris, Richard S., *Bum Rap on American Cities*, Englewood Cliffs, N.J.: Prentice-Hall, 1978.
Mumford, Lewis, *The Culture of Cities*, New York: Harcourt Brace Jovanovich, 1970.
On-Site Generation: Site Energy-Using Functions, New Haven: Earth Metabolic Design, Inc., 1981.
Okagaki, Alan, *County Energy Plan Guidebook: Creating a Renewable Energy Plan*, Fairfax, Virginia: Institute for Ecological Policies, 1979.
Ostrom, Elinor, et. al., *Community Organization and the Provision of Public Services*, Beverly Hills: Sage Publications, 1973.
Peterson, Rein, *Small Business: Building a Balanced Economy*, Ontario: Press Porcepic, 1977.
Poole, Robert W., Jr., *Cutting Back City Hall*, New York: Universe Books, 1980.
Pratten, C. F., *Economies of Scale in Manufacturing*, Cambridge, England: Cambridge Univ. Press, 1975.
Quarles, John, *"Federal Regulations of New Industrial Plants,"* Washington, D.C.: self-published, 1979.
Rainbook: Resources for Appropriate Technology, New York: Schocken Books, 1977.
Ridgeway, James, *Energy Efficient Community Planning*, Emmaus, P.A.: The JG Press, 1979.
Rifkin, Jeremy and Barber, Randy, *The North Will Rise Again*, Boston: Beacon Press, 1970.
Saalman, Howard, *Medieval Cities*, New York: George Braziller, 1968.
Sanger, John M. Associates and Epstein, Peter, B., *Municipal Solar Utilities in California*, Sacramento: California Energy Commission, 1981.
Scherer, F. M., et. al., *The Economics of Multi-Plant Operation: An International Comparison Study*, Cambridge: Harvard Economic Studies, 1975.
Seldman, Neil N., *Economic Feasibility of Recycling*, Washington, D.C.: Institute for Local Self-Reliance, June, 1978.
Stein, Barry, A., *Size, Efficiency and Community Enterprise*, Cambridge: Center for Community Economic Development, 1975.

Stein, Barry A. and Hodax, Mark B., *Competitive Scale in Manufacturing: The Case of Consumer Goods*, Cambridge: Center for Community Economic Development, 1976.

Stein, Richard G., *Architecture and Energy: Conserving Energy Through Rational Design*, Garden City, New York: Anchor Press, 1977.

Stephens, G. Ross and Olson, Gerald W., *Pass-Through Federal Aid and Interlevel Finance in the American Federal System 1957-1977*, Two Volumes, Kansas City: University of Missouri-Kansas City, August 1, 1979.

Stocks, Anthony H., *Considerations of Scale on Providing State and Local Public Goods*, West Virginia Univ., Center for Appalachian Studies and Development, 1968.

Tiger, Michael E. and Levy, Madeleine R., *Law and the Rise of Capitalism*, New York: Monthly Review Press, 1977.

Tomasi, Tom, *Local Energy Initiatives: A Second Look: A Survey of Cities and Counties in California*, 1981, Sacramento: Office of Appropriate Technology, 1981.

Vernon, Raymond, *The Changing Economic Function of the Central City*, New York: CED, 1959.

Williams, Charles B., *Contracting for City Services: An Annotated Bibliography*, Norman, Oklahoma: Bureau of Government Research, University of Oklahoma, July, 1980.

Wilson, Peter, *The Future of Dallas' Capital Plant*, Washington, D.C.: The Urban Institute, 1980.

Wolfe, David B., *Condominium and Homeowner Associations That Work: On Paper and In Action*, Washington, D.C.: The Urban Land Institute, 1978.

Yates, Douglas, *The Ungovernable City: The Politics of Urban Problems and Policy Making*, Cambridge: MIT Press, 1977.

Zwerdling, Daniel, *Democracy at Work: A Guide to Workplace Ownership, Participation and Self-Management Experiments in the U.S. and Europe*, Washington, D.C.: Association for Self-Management, 1978.